W9-CFV-579

ISLANDS OF HOPE

ALSO BY PHILLIP MANNING

Afoot in the South: Walks in the Natural Areas of North Carolina

Palmetto Journal: Walks in the Natural Areas of South Carolina

Orange Blossom Trails: Walks in the Natural Areas of Florida

ISLANDS OF HOPE

by Phillip Manning

Phillip Manning

John F. Blair, Publisher
Winston-Salem, North Carolina

ILLUSTRATIONS BY DIANE MANNING

DESIGN BY DEBRA LONG HAMPTON

PRINTED AND BOUND BY R. R. DONNELLEY & SONS

The paper in this book meets the guidelines
for permanence and durability
of the Committee on Production Guidelines
for Book Longevity of the Council on Library Resources.

Library of Congress Cataloging-in-Publication Data

Manning, Phillip, 1936–

Islands of hope / by Phillip Manning.

p.   cm.

Includes bibliographical references (p.   ) and index.

ISBN 0-89587-183-1 (alk. paper)

1. Wildlife refuges—North America.   2. Wildlife conservation—North America.

I. Title.

QL84.M35   1999   99–32139

333.95'416'097—dc21

This one's for the kids, Robin and Michael

Contents

INTRODUCTION

Wildlife Conservation in North America   3

CHAPTER 1

A Perfect Park

Bonaire Marine Park, Bonaire, Netherlands Antilles   11

CHAPTER 2

Ancient Cypresses, Young Storks

Corkscrew Swamp Sanctuary, Florida   30

CHAPTER 3

Where Butterflies Go

El Rosario Monarch Butterfly Preserve, Michoacán, Mexico   49

CHAPTER 4

Shorebirds and Crabs

Cape May National Wildlife Refuge, New Jersey   65

CHAPTER 5

The Surviving Auk

Machias Seal Island, New Brunswick, Canada   83

CHAPTER 6

Goose Lake, Swan Lake

Mattamuskeet National Wildlife Refuge, North Carolina   98

CHAPTER 7

Where the Buffalo Roam

Tallgrass Prairie Preserve, Oklahoma   *114*

CHAPTER 8

The Antelope Dilemma

Hart Mountain National Antelope Refuge, Oregon   *130*

CHAPTER 9

The Science of Muddling Through

Bon Secour National Wildlife Refuge, Alabama   *148*

CHAPTER 10

Where the Wild Goose Goes

Horicon National Wildlife Refuge, Wisconsin   *162*

CHAPTER 11

Putting It All Together   *177*

ACKNOWLEDGMENTS   *187*

APPENDIX

For More Information   *189*

BIBLIOGRAPHY   *191*

INDEX   204

For the green prehuman earth is the mystery we were chosen to solve, a guide to the birthplace of our spirit, but it is slipping away.

Edward O. Wilson,
The Diversity of Life

$\mathcal{W}$ildlife Conservation in North America

THE DESTRUCTION OF North America's wildlife started soon after the first humans walked across the Beringian land bridge. Those early Americans may have hunted the mastodon and the mammoth to extinction.

The slaughter accelerated with the arrival of Europeans. The great auk and the Labrador duck soon succumbed. Bison were hunted nearly to extinction, as were fur seals and beavers. By the beginning of the twentieth century, even the now-ubiquitous white-tailed deer and gray squirrel were scarce in the eastern United States, and the passenger pigeon was in its final throes. The prevailing attitude of the time was summed up by a hunter: "The good Lord put us here and the Good Book says, 'Man shall have dominion over all creatures.' They're ourn to use."

But new ideas about the natural world were beginning to blow across the land. In 1854, Thoreau praised the virtues of wildness in *Walden*, portraying nature as a web of life in which mankind was member rather than ruler. Five years later came *The Origin of Species*. Darwin said explicitly what Thoreau alluded to. "Animals," he wrote, "are our fellow brethren in suffering, disease and death." Soon afterward, the United States began to act to preserve its natural heritage.

The first step in North America toward protecting land in its natural state was an unprecedented act of the United States Congress. In 1864, President Abraham Lincoln signed legislation deeding Yosemite Valley and the great Mariposa Grove of ancient sequoias to the state of California for "public use, resort and recreation." Eight years later, Congress approved more precedent-setting legislation; it established Yellowstone, the world's first national park.

Canada followed suit in 1887, creating Rocky Mountains Park, which was later renamed Banff National Park. A few years later, urged on by a stubborn conservationist named John Muir, Congress made Yosemite a national park, forever protecting its "natural curiosities or wonders, and their retention in their natural condition."

These early parks offered only limited protection for wildlife. They were created as "a pleasuring ground for the benefit and enjoyment of people." It wasn't until 1894 that Congress protected some of the wildlife in national parks and only much later that it extended that protection to predators.

In 1900, in one of the first actions aimed solely at conserving wildlife, the organization that later became the National Audubon Society hired wardens to guard the gulls on Matinicus Rock, a remote island off the Maine coast.

Three years later, President Theodore Roosevelt set aside the first federal land for the exclusive purpose of protecting wildlife—a three-and-a-half-acre island in the Indian River delta a few miles south of Melbourne, Florida. The island was a breeding ground for pelicans, and as private yachts sailed by, passengers would blast away at the slow-flying birds. The pelicans weren't killed to be eaten, or even retrieved from where they fell. They were shot simply for "sport."

The American Ornithologists' Union recommended that the island be designated a bird refuge. When its letter reached Roosevelt, he acted with characteristic speed and boldness. "It is hereby ordered," he wrote, "that Pelican Island in Indian River . . . is hereby reserved and set apart for the use of the Department of Agriculture as a preserve and breeding ground for native birds." Theodore Roosevelt had established the United States' first national wildlife refuge.

In the next few years, the national system of refuges grew rapidly. By the time Roosevelt left office, he had protected fifty-three sites. The Audubon Society also expanded, as more and more people came to realize that the wildlife of the young nation, which had once seemed unlimited, was not inexhaustible.

Canada was reaching the same conclusion. In 1918, it joined the United States in partially protecting migratory birds. Four years later, it established Wood Buffalo National Park, the largest park in North America. Mexico dedicated its first park in 1917. This was a major stride for a country about which conservationist Miguel Alvarez del Toro later said, "It is difficult to find a country less interested in the conservation of its natural resources than Mexico."

But the well-meaning conservationists of the early twentieth century lacked scientific knowledge, and some of their practices were questionable at best and harmful at worst. Predator elimination, fire suppression, and flood control often hurt the very resource they wanted to protect. The conservationists who led the sanctuary movement knew where they wanted to go, but they needed a map to show them how to get there. The newly developing science of ecology would provide that map.

The term *ecology* was coined in 1869 by German biologist Ernst Haeckel. But ecology—literally, "the study of organisms at home"—wasn't recognized as a science until about 1900. Practically, it came to mean the study of how organisms interact with their environment.

The nascent science took a leap forward in 1927, when a young Oxford graduate, Charles Elton, published *Animal Ecology*. It was an ambitious, groundbreaking book that attempted to turn natural history into a science. In it, Elton introduced the concepts of the "pyramid of numbers" and the food web.

By the late 1940s, British-born Yale professor G. Evelyn Hutchinson was advocating a mathematical approach to ecology. He also added evolutionary biology to the science. To understand an ecosystem, he said, one must understand the evolutionary forces that created it. The new science was on its way to becoming an established discipline.

With conservationists leading the charge and ecologists directing it, public and private refuge systems continued to grow. In the United States, this expansion got a boost in 1934, when President Franklin Roosevelt appointed Jay Norwood "Ding" Darling, a dedicated conservationist and Pulitzer Prize–winning cartoonist, to head the Biological Survey, the predecessor of the United States Fish and Wildlife Service. Darling scrambled hard for scarce federal money during the Depression and added four million acres to the wildlife refuge system. He also started the duck-stamp program and, making use of his artistic abilities, designed the first stamp.

Conservationists realized that refuges alone couldn't adequately protect wildlife; legislation would also be required. Although closed seasons on birds had been established by some states as early as the eighteenth century, there were few federal laws aimed at conserving wildlife until Ding Darling created the duck stamp. It was, in effect, a national hunting license, and it helped establish the federal government's obligation to defend wildlife. Six years later, Congress passed laws that protected the bald eagle in all states.

In the activist 1960s, spurred by the publication of Rachel Carson's classic book, *Silent Spring*—a call to arms about the dangers of pesticides—the pace of environmental legislation picked up. Over a ten-year period beginning in 1963, Congress passed the Clean Air Act, the Wilderness Act, the National Environmental Policy Act, water pollution and pesticide control acts, and, finally, the Endangered Species Act in 1973. At last, the conservation movement had some powerful legal weapons in its arsenal.

Mexico and Canada also made significant progress. Canada created several new national parks and, in 1947, formed the Canadian Wildlife Service. Mexico passed pollution control laws in 1971 and established the Mariposa Preserve for monarch butterflies in 1980.

Ecology grew during this period, too, and some say it splintered. Robert McIntosh, the distinguished ecologist from the University of Notre

Dame, has counted dozens of what he calls "hyphenated disciplines": population-ecology, behavioral-ecology, restoration-ecology, etc. New words were created as researchers tried to come up with apt descriptions of their work—ecophysiology, for example, bioscience, and many others.

Notable among these new fields was island biogeography. The theoretical underpinnings of the discipline came from a book entitled *The Theory of Island Biogeography*, written in 1967 by two highly respected scientists, Robert H. MacArthur and Edward O. Wilson.

MacArthur had a master's degree in mathematics, but he turned to ecology for his Ph.D., working for Hutchinson at Yale. Following Hutchinson's footsteps, MacArthur wanted to construct mathematical models and turn the hitherto descriptive science of ecology into a predictive one. By the time he accepted a teaching job at Princeton, he had already met and shared ideas with the man who was to be his coauthor.

Ed Wilson was a Southerner, a naturalist at heart, who had lost an eye to the sharp spine of a pinfish. He had a consuming interest in ants and a bright, questioning mind. He was also a fine writer who later won two Pulitzer Prizes for nonfiction. He was already a professor at Harvard when he decided that island biogeography was ripe for a sounder theoretical base. With MacArthur's mathematical bent and Wilson's writing skills and field experience with ant populations on islands, the two men were a good fit.

The Theory of Island Biogeography is filled with pages of hairy-looking differential equations and graphs that show how the rates of immigration and extinction on an island eventually reach equilibrium, leaving the island with a predictable number of species. The relationship that the theory aims to explain is stated concisely at the end of chapter 2: "The number of species on a given island is usually approximately related to the area of the island."

The authors were well aware of what that statement meant for a planet whose natural areas were being isolated from one another by agriculture and development. "The same principles [of island biogeography] apply," they wrote, "and will continue to apply to an accelerating extent in the future, to formerly continuous natural habitats now being broken up by the encroachment of civilization." In other words, natural areas were becoming islands. And the smaller the islands, the fewer species they could support. One could therefore expect to see an increasing number of extinctions as natural areas were further fragmented and slowly relaxed toward equilibrium.

The book stimulated yet another subdiscipline of ecology: conservation biology. The first conference on conservation biology was held in San Diego in 1978. From it came a book, *Conservation Biology: An Evolutionary-Ecological Perspective*, edited by Michael Soulé and Bruce Wilcox. In the first chapter, they defined the term: "Conservation biology is a mission-oriented discipline comprising both pure and applied science."

In practice, conservation biology became a discipline that developed and used science to preserve biodiversity, a mission its practitioners undertook with evangelical fervor. The cause was an important one, and the mood was less than optimistic. "The green mantle of earth is now being ravaged and pillaged in a frenzy of exploitation by a mushrooming mass of humans and bulldozers," the authors wrote. "Never in the 500 million years of terrestrial evolution has this mantle we call the biosphere been under such savage attack."

One way to blunt the attack on biodiversity was to create nature preserves. Conservation biologists were quick to apply island biogeography to the design of preserves. Perhaps the most influential paper on the subject was written by Jared Diamond in 1975. Although Diamond was a physiologist, he was also an accomplished field ornithologist, and he quickly grasped the implications of island biogeography. (He was a good writer, too, who—like E. O. Wilson—later won a Pulitzer Prize for nonfiction.)

In "The Island Dilemma: Lessons of Modern Biogeographic Studies for the Design of Natural Reserves," Diamond used the theory of island biogeography to produce a set of principles to guide the design of nature preserves. "A large reserve is better than a small reserve . . . for two reasons," he wrote. "The large reserve can hold more species at equilibrium, and it will have lower extinction rates."

Not everybody agreed with Diamond's conclusions. Daniel Simberloff and Lawrence Abele shot back a dissenting view in a January 1976 paper in the prestigious journal *Science*. They said that "a cluster of small refuges might be expected to have more species than a single large one." Though they couched their concluding sentence in the cautious language of academese, its meaning was clear: "In sum, the broad generalizations that have been reported [by Diamond] are based on limited and insufficiently validated theory."

This paper was the first skirmish in a war between those ecologists who believed that a few large refuges were superior to many small ones and those who believed that many small refuges were the way to go. So widespread was this disagreement that it became known by the acronym SLOSS (Single Large Or Several Small). The SLOSS battles dominated ecology for years and were ably chronicled by David Quammen in *The Song of the Dodo*.

The issue was never really settled, but most ecologists have now put the acrimony behind them. When in the real world, they ask, do we actually have a choice between a single large preserve and several small ones? Soulé (who supported Diamond's single-large views) and Simberloff (the chief spokesman for the several-small side) got together on a paper in 1986. In it, they reached a conclusion with which virtually every ecologist could agree: "Nature reserves should be as large as possible, and there should be many of them."

Although few naturalists today believe that we have enough reserves, big or little, the work of ecologists, conservationists, and governments has given us an impressive collection of wildlife preserves. The United States alone operates over 500 national wildlife refuges covering 91 million acres. It protects animals and habitats on another 83 million acres in the national parks system. National forests also offer some protection for wildlife. In Canada, wildlife refuges and national parks protect migratory waterfowl, seabirds, bison, caribou, and seals. Mexico has established numerous national parks and has shown a heightened sensitivity to environmental concerns. Most Caribbean countries have also set aside parks and preserves for wildlife, many of which protect coral-reef ecosystems and the abundant marine life they harbor. Several nonprofit organizations have established substantial refuge systems of their own. The National Audubon Society owns over 100 sanctuaries, and The Nature Conservancy operates an astounding 1,650.

Collectively, these sanctuaries have sparked a resurgence of wildlife in North America, and they shelter an amazing number of animals. Millions of monarch butterflies and hundreds of thousands of shorebirds, Canada geese, and other species owe their existence to these "islands of hope." Without these protected patches of green in a landscape of farm fields, parking lots, and suburban sprawl, many species—from bison and pronghorns to wood storks and razor-billed auks—would be far less numerous, and others would likely be extinct.

In this book, we will visit ten sanctuaries—each managed by a government or a nonprofit organization—that offer crucial protection for wildlife in four North American countries. We will investigate the animals and ecosystems they were designed to protect. We will talk with the people who run them to learn how they use conservation laws and the science of ecology in their work. We will explore how refuges are created and how that plays a role in their success. At Bonaire Marine Park in the Netherlands Antilles, for example, the farsighted conservationists who founded the park established stringent regulations that have kept that island's coral reefs pristine. But the formation of El Rosario Monarch Butterfly Preserve in Mexico imposed economic hardships on neighboring campesinos that have led to resentment and poaching. We will also examine the still-lingering question of refuge size. And finally, we will explore the threats facing North America's sanctuaries as we begin the twenty-first century.

$\mathscr{A}$ Perfect Park

Bonaire Marine Park, Bonaire, Netherlands Antilles

WHAT DO YOU DO when the temperature dips and your friends Jim and Martha Foght head for their winter home in the Caribbean? Well, you can stew in the green juices of your envy or go into convulsions of sun-deprived self-pity. Or you can invite yourself down for a week. Which is how I got acquainted with the island of Bonaire.

I start today as I start every day on the island: drinking coffee in my bathing suit and watching perky, yellow-breasted banana quits swirl from feeder to feeder on the Foghts' patio. Then I climb down the ladder that leads from their backyard to the sea, slip on mask and flippers, and slide into the warm, turquoise waters of Bonaire Marine Park, one of North America's best-preserved sanctuaries.

I snorkel over white sand and coral rubble. Silvery needlefish hang motionless at the water's surface, and trunkfish peck away at the algae that coats the coral litter. The water deepens, and the landscape beneath my mask changes to great racks of tan elkhorn coral spotted with red algae. In the blue-green haze ahead, a barrier of tightly packed elkhorn coral marks the reef crest. A stoplight parrotfish, its coarse scales ablaze with yellows, greens, and blues, crunches dead coral, then excretes a puff of white sediment, the raw material of the Caribbean's white-sand beaches.

Scattered boulders of brain coral mix with staghorn and elkhorn coral. But these are only the obvious species of corals; dozens of others live here, too, from fire coral to flower coral. There are also sponges, sea fans, and lamp shells. And in the crevices and interstices of coral skeletons live worms and urchins, shrimps and crabs. Schools of electric-blue chromis swarm through this jungle, and wrasses are everywhere. Shells once inhabited by living invertebrates lie passively on the sea floor. As usual, this conflation of life and death reminds me of an old-growth forest, where decay and rebirth dance together in a waltz so intricate that it bewilders the eye.

I head for deeper water. The reef crest, a jumble of jagged corals bound together by encrusting coralline algae and fire coral, rises from the sea floor to within a foot or two of my pale, vulnerable belly. I kick harder and pass over without mishap. Then the reef falls away. Beyond it is blue, deep ocean.

I turn ninety degrees and swim parallel to the reef. It's hard to believe that this massive structure could be built by tiny polyps of coral, which reminds me of something else coral reefs have in common with old-growth forests: both are highly complex ecosystems that take centuries to develop but can be destroyed in the blink of an eye.

Coral reefs are in trouble the world over. In an irruption probably stimulated by excessive nutrient runoffs, crown-of-thorns starfish are devouring Australia's Great Barrier Reef; pollution, sedimentation, and anchor damage are degrading Florida's reefs; the cyanide used to stun fish to collect them for tropical-aquarium enthusiasts is poisoning corals in the Philippines; and unusually high water temperatures are bleaching coral reefs around the globe. Before these became serious problems, though, Bonaire was vigorously protecting its reefs. And the island's farsighted approach to conservation has paid off; its reefs remain pristine.

As is often the case with conservation success stories, geography and a few determined people played major roles in preserving this ecosystem.

Bonaire is a 111-square-mile, comma-shaped patch of arid land lying about 50 miles north of Venezuela. The comma shelters Klein Bonaire, a much smaller, uninhabited island. Both islands are ringed with reefs. Because Bonaire is south of the hurricane belt, its reefs rarely suffer the damage those storms can inflict. Less geographically lucky sites, such as the Society Islands in the Pacific, regularly have their reefs devastated by hurricanes.

Donal Stewart, known to all Bonaireans as "Captain Don," came to the island in 1962. He was looking for a good place to dive, and because the undisturbed reefs of Bonaire suited him perfectly, he stayed. He was poor at the time, down to smoking cigarette butts and eating canned cranberry sauce for supper. But as he wrote in his memoirs, he wasn't broke: "Sixty-three cents ain't broke. Should a been around during the depression. Zero was broke."

After he recovered financially, Captain Don opened the first dive shop on the island and soon realized that Bonaire could become a popular scuba-diving site. He also realized that hordes of divers anchoring on the reefs could harm the very resource that brought them to the island. Consequently, while diving on Bonaire was still in its infancy, Captain Don placed the first mooring buoy on the island's reefs. And as diving picked up, the island government was quick to understand the value of the reefs in attracting tourists.

Bonaire is one of the Netherlands Antilles (as are Curaçao, Saba, St. Eustatius, and St. Maarten), which are a territory of the Netherlands. The Netherlands Antilles are governed by a democratically elected parliament, but an island council manages Bonaire's local affairs. The council meets in Kralendijk, the island's capital and only sizable town. In 1971, the council banned spearfishing, an act comparable to forbidding deer hunting in Michigan. In 1975, it stopped all coral collecting. Four years later, helped by a grant from the World Wildlife Fund, Bonaire Marine Park was established.

From the very beginning, the park took a no-nonsense approach to conservation. First, its management decided to protect all of Bonaire's reefs, even though development and diving threatened only a few. This made enforcement of the park's rules easier. "For example," explained the park's first manager, Tom van't Hof, "if coral collecting is prohibited in the marine park and the park only included the reefs of Klein Bonaire, a diver caught outside his hotel unloading some fresh trunks of black coral could allege to have collected outside the park boundaries. By applying the same regulations to all reefs, this is not possible."

Today, the marine park encompasses the sea bottom and overlying waters from the high-water mark to the sixty-meter (two-hundred-foot) depth contour. Anchoring, spearfishing, and live-shell and coral collecting are forbidden; divers and snorkelers are warned to avoid even touching the corals; and Captain Don's one mooring buoy has grown into a string of seventy-five public dive moorings along the leeward shore of the island. The number of divers has grown, too, but thanks to the conservation measures pushed by Captain Don, Tom van't Hof, and others—and supported by the enlightened citizens of Bonaire—the reefs are essentially unchanged.

The next morning, I'm back in the sea again, snorkeling over the reef. I love this ecosystem, the otherworldliness of its extensive and ever-changing cast of characters. Charles Birkeland, a scientist at the University of Guam, maintains that "coral reefs have the greatest species diversity per square meter of any community on Earth." Of course, it is this aspect of coral reefs that makes them so popular; divers would be rare if all sea bottoms were sand.

But the complexity of the ecosystem makes it almost impossible to grasp what's going on. Even food-chain relationships, which are often simple on land, are complicated here. As if to underscore the point, a spectacular parrotfish, a glowing blue male, appears beneath me, biting enthusiastically at the coral.

Members of the family Scaridae, parrotfish are large (up to four feet long), blunt headed, and brightly colored, with large scales and fused teeth. Their dazzling hues and beaklike mouth apparently reminded some heat-addled tropical explorer of a parrot, hence their common name. Parrotfish hang around coral reefs throughout the world. Males and females of the same species are often quite different in appearance, and young parrotfish have a disturbing habit of changing sexes and colors. To complicate matters further, some sexually mature female parrotfish undergo a final growth spurt in which they change colors and sexes again. They also grow pugnacious. These oversized fish are like bodybuilders on steroids, and they go by a name bodybuilders would appreciate: *supermales*. However, the name is only partially accurate; supermales are often poor spawners.

This confusion of colors, sizes, and sexes has caused some folks to surmise that there are far more species of parrotfish than actually exist. In a Smithsonian Institution monograph, Leonard Schultz found 364 species of parrotfish listed in the literature, but his own research led him to conclude that there are actually only 80 species in the world. Consequently, figuring out which parrotfish species live where mightily frustrates ichthyologists. As Schultz noted somberly, "So much misidentification is prevalent for parrotfishes in the ichthyological literature that at present the geographical distribution of each species of parrotfish cannot be worked out in detail."

The confusion is understandable; parrotfish are hard to identify. For example, I'm reasonably certain that the bright aqua fish below me is a blue parrotfish, *Scarus coerleus*, a plentiful fish in Bonaire's waters. However, supermale yellowtail parrotfish are close to the same color. And though yellowtails are rarer here, there's no way to know for sure which species this is, short of killing it and examining its teeth, scales, and fin spines. And I'd never kill a fish just to learn its name; a live fish of uncertain species is more interesting than a properly identified dead one.

Regardless of species, though, all parrotfish have two things in common: ravenous appetites and bad table manners. They constantly chomp away at the reefs that shelter them, tearing off chunks of coral with an audible crunching sound, pulverizing them, and expelling calcium carbonate. A single parrotfish can consume a pound of limestone in a year. Since the reefs teem with parrotfish, the wear and tear on corals is substantial. So impressed were ecologists by the damage parrotfish (and other organisms) inflict on reefs that they coined a term for the process: *bioerosion*.

But in this complicated ecosystem, nothing is as it seems. For all their munching and crunching on the reefs, parrotfish do little damage to living coral polyps. They are merely grazing on the algae that coats the coral skeletons. The scraping of their beaks only incidentally erodes the reefs.

Incidental or not, parrotfish can weaken the structure that supports live corals. So it would appear that they are harmful to the corals, albeit unintentionally. But again, appearances deceive. Without parrotfish (and other herbivores) to graze the foliose algae that coats the reefs, the algae would overgrow them and kill the corals. Thus, coral reefs owe their very existence to parrotfish and other algae grazers.

The parrotfish below me doesn't look like the savior of anything. It slides in and out of crevices, appearing and disappearing in the gray-green reef, pecking at coral and doing what millennia of natural selection have programmed it to do. Probably a hundred different organisms are within my view. Microscopic borers, crabs, sponges, and sea stars are all leading shadowy, complicated lives beyond my mask. And each species is playing a part in a great Darwinian epic directed by the reef.

The incredible species diversity is what makes coral-reef ecosystems so interesting to ecologists. The complicated interrelationships among species—like that among parrotfish, algae, and corals—are challenging to figure out. Complex ecosystems like this one can be surprisingly resilient when they are intact, but after they have been altered by man, they heal slowly, if at all.

Take, for example, the strange case of the long-spined sea urchin, *Diadema antillarum*. This sea urchin is about four inches long and resembles a black pincushion abristle with long, sharp needles. It lives in crevices in coral reefs and grazes on algae and occasionally live corals.

In 1983, the long-spined sea urchins of the Caribbean began to die. The mysterious disease, whose source was never pinpointed, spread rapidly, eventually killing over 90 percent of the population. In many spots, mortality was 100 percent. Within weeks, foliose algae growing on and around the reefs increased by 50 percent. After several years, many corals were overgrown and dying. None of this was a surprise to ecologists; the feeding habits of these sea urchins were well known.

What was surprising was the small effect that the die-off had on healthy reefs, such as Bonaire's. As with other islands in the region, Bonaire's urchins succumbed to the disease. Its corals, however, survived with little damage. The reason was the reefs' robust populations of parrotfish and other herbivorous fish, which enjoyed boom times in the absence of the competing urchins. The islands that suffered the most were those where fishermen had overharvested algae-grazing fish.

This kind of complexity has made scientists understandably cautious about tampering with the natural processes of coral reefs. Mark Hixon, a zoologist at Oregon State University, summed up this attitude in *Life and Death of Coral Reefs*: "Reef systems may be too complicated to allow us to predict explicit outcomes of human activities . . . [so] managers should cast a skeptical and cautious eye on proposals to strongly alter the abundance of any coral reef inhabitant."

Snorkeling toward home in the crystal-clear water above the reef, it is easy to agree with Dr. Hixon about the complicated nature of these ecosystems. Some form of life covers every surface of the reef below me. Most prominent are the corals: the ubiquitous fields of elkhorn and staghorn; great mountains of star coral and little gobbets of golf-ball coral; tube, bush, and scroll corals; and others I can't identify. Though the swarms of brightly colored fish are the main attraction for divers, the corals are the base on which this ecosystem rests. It is the corals that build the reefs, and it is the reefs that supply the crannies and nooks where fish hide. The reefs also provide the solid structure on which algae grow, and they protect all of their inhabitants, including the coral polyps themselves, from predators and the swirling currents of the open sea.

In fact, reefs are an ideal environment for many organisms. So useful are they that the earliest known life on our planet formed reefs.

Stromatolites are stubby columns of finely layered limestone fifteen or so inches tall. They bear an uncanny resemblance to a stack of very thin pancakes. Geologists have long been aware of stromatolites but disagreed about their origin. Some thought they were fossilized structures created by living creatures; others thought they were merely unusual rock formations. The question was an important one because some stromatolites are ancient. In Australia, scientists have discovered stromatolites that are 3.5 billion years old, which means they were formed only a few hundred million years after the earth's crust solidified. If living organisms created them, then they would be the earliest form of life known.

The nature of fossilized stromatolites wasn't determined until the early 1960s, when a geology graduate student named Brian Logan discovered *living* stromatolites in the shallow waters of Shark Bay off the coast of

Australia. Although modern stromatolites had been investigated as early as 1933, those at Shark Bay were remarkable because they bore an unmistakable resemblance to fossilized stromatolites. The new evidence swayed most scientists, who now generally accept that fossilized stromatolites were created by living organisms.

Living stromatolites (and presumably ancient ones) are composed of thin layers of algal mats. The top layer is a sticky surface of photosynthetic cyanobacteria once called blue-green algae and known colloquially as pond scum. As sediment builds up on the gummy uppermost layer, the algae migrate upward, toward the life-giving sun, leaving an oxygen-depleted zone in which anaerobic microbes thrive. Over centuries, this process produces a finely layered stromatolite.

Stromatolites are found throughout the fossil record, but they became less abundant half a billion years ago, and living stromatolites are rare. The reason for their decline was the rise of multicellular invertebrates such as snails, which grazed on cyanobacteria. These grazers reduced the abundance of stromatolite-forming bacteria. However, for three billion years, cyanobacteria ruled the earth. Their most important legacy is the oxygen in our atmosphere, without which we could not exist. But they left us something else, too. As we shall see, the light-seeking urge that enabled the cyanobacteria to create the ancient stromatolites lives on in today's reef-building corals.

I am sitting on a deck behind the Foghts' house, perhaps ten feet above the Caribbean. The water beneath me is as clear as the gin in my glass. Trunkfish and parrotfish dart across patches of white sand to peck at the algae that grow on the rocks and corals, then vanish into hidey-holes in the reef. The muted waves whip up miniature whirlwinds of sand that swirl across the sea floor like dust devils across a desert. Comparing a coral reef to a desert is not as farfetched as it seems. In one surprising way, this richly biodiverse ecosystem resembles a desert.

One of the great attractions of tropical seas is their combination of clarity and color. The turquoise waters of the shallows change abruptly to the royal blue of deep water on the far side of the reef. The blue is a reflection of the sky, and the shallows appear turquoise because of the white-sand bottom. But the sky is blue everywhere on earth, so why are temperate and polar seas often green and turbid, instead of blue and clear? The answer is that cool waters teem with tiny green plants called phytoplankton, which are far less abundant in warm, tropical waters. Phytoplankton is food for microscopic animals called zooplankton. Together, these tiny organisms (along with some sediments) create the cloudy, discolored seas to the north and provide food for everything from barnacles to blue whales.

This dearth of plankton is what makes coral reefs resemble deserts; reefs are low in food, just as deserts are low in moisture—and both are requirements for life. But plants and animals abound on reefs, in contrast to the sparseness of life in a desert. How this cornucopia of life thrives in the low-nutrient tropical waters that bathe the coral reefs was a mystery until recently. It was solved when scientists began to understand more about the creatures that create this ecosystem: the corals.

Coral polyps appear to be simple creatures with simple lifestyles. Their bodies consist mainly of tentacles to capture food, a mouth to devour it, and a digestive tract to process it. During the day, polyps usually hunker down in the limestone cups they build to protect themselves. At night, they extend sticky tentacles to capture any zooplankton that float by. But scientists calculated that polyps could obtain only a small fraction of the food they need to survive from the nutrient-poor waters where they live. Like the engineers who proved bumblebees couldn't fly, biologists proved that corals couldn't exist.

Of course, corals *do* exist, and no one was more aware of that than the scientists who studied them. The logjam was broken in the 1920s when members of a British expedition to the Great Barrier Reef showed that chlorophyll-containing algae lived in the bodies of coral polyps. Some scientists suspected the algae were providing food for the polyps.

Today, we know their suspicions were correct. Like true plants, the symbiotic algae (known as zooxanthellae) that reside in the bodies of coral polyps convert sunlight and carbon dioxide into oxygen, water, and sugars by photosynthesis. And corals, like all animals, require oxygen, water, and sugars to live. Also like other animals, they produce carbon dioxide and ammonia (which is mostly nitrogen) as waste products. The result is a wonderfully efficient system of recycling. The algae supply the polyps with oxygen, water, and sugars; the polyps supply the algae carbon dioxide and a safe haven where they can soak up sunlight. And the ammonia given off by the polyps helps keep the algae healthy in exactly the same way that nitrogen fertilizer helps lawns to flourish. It is, all in all, a very neat arrangement.

The coral polyps of a reef are merely a veneer of life less than an inch thick, supported by a calcium carbonate skeleton. As it turns out, the algae embedded in the coral also enhance calcification, thus playing an important role in the formation of the reef itself. An acre of coral, abetted by the ubiquitous algae in the polyps, can produce forty tons of limestone in a year. Over time, this productivity can create impressive structures. Some Pacific reefs are over four thousand feet thick, and Australia's Great Barrier Reef is nearly thirteen hundred *miles* long.

Like the blue-green algae that created the ancient stromatolites, the simple, single-cell algae found in the bodies of coral polyps played a key role in forming modern reefs, the most massive structures created by any organism. Algae don't rule the world as they once did, but on the reefs, they still do the heavy lifting.

On our last day in Bonaire, I join Jim and Martha for a long snorkel down the reef that protects Klein Bonaire, the small island that lies a mile east of Kralendijk. The sea is calm, the sun bright and hot. I jump off the boat, clear my mask, and drift into a coralline world. The reef starts practically on the shore, then drops off steeply to a hundred feet. Orange elephant-ear and purple tube sponges decorate the jumble of corals that covers the wall. Martha, an excellent naturalist, points out leaf coral, wire coral, and mountainous star coral. A hawksbill turtle passes only a few yards in front of my mask, swimming effortlessly with leopard-spotted flippers. Martha follows him into deeper water.

Despite my vow to be more businesslike today, to concentrate on the corals—which I keep reminding myself are the heart of this ecosystem— the fish distract me. And a shark I spot lazing along beneath me is especially distracting. I am determined to identify it. From my bathing suit, I pull out the plastic "Fish-at-a-Glance" card I carry with me. The card has drawings of the common fish of the Netherlands Antilles, from butterfly fish to wrasses. But no sharks. My guess is the artist didn't want to advertise that sharks swim among the Caribbean's tourist-attracting reefs.

The shark is about three or four feet long, a gray torpedo that would be menacing if it paid any attention to me. But it doesn't. This indifference to humans is characteristic of the sharks I've encountered while snorkeling. Only once, in the Bahamas, have I ever seen one act threateningly. A nine-foot nurse shark suddenly appeared behind my wife, Diane, and closed the gap until it was only a few feet from her flippers. I began splashing toward her and yelling underwater. The shark sped away without out Diane's ever seeing it, and after she surfaced, she accused me of making the whole thing up.

So even though sharks don't overly concern me, I do believe in keeping an eye on them. And it is only when this one lounges away from the reef, still unidentified, and fades away into the blue smoke of deep water that I focus on the myriad other fish that surround me. Bright, colorful shapes flit around the reef, and as usual, I forget my vow to pay attention to the corals.

A cloud of silvery palometas materializes over the reef and engulfs me. For years, I scoured Florida's sun-blasted flats, trying in vain to catch the palometa's larger cousin, the permit. The permits apparently passed on their low opinion of my fishing prowess to these palometas, because they show absolutely no fear. They swim unconcernedly within inches of my mask before vanishing as suddenly as they appeared.

The current carries me over the heart of the reef. Soon, two French angelfish, perhaps the most spectacular reef species in the Caribbean, join me. They float along a few feet below me and slightly to my left, giving me a perfect view. They are discus shaped, maybe a foot long. One of them seems almost as interested in me as I am in it, tilting itself in the water to watch me with an eerie, yellow-ringed eye. Every scale on its midsection is blue with a yellow edge. The whole fish resembles a dark cloth sprinkled with gold dust. And like an Escher drawing, the colors seem to metamorphose, changing from blue to yellow and blue, then back to blue.

When we reach deeper water, the angelfish scoot back to safety. A trio of barracudas hangs motionless in the blue stillness beyond. I turn and swim toward the reef.

Shimmering schools of black-and-yellow sergeant majors swim leisurely over the dark reef. I spot butterfly fish, filefish, and trunkfish; damselfish, triggerfish, and parrotfish; and several species of blue-and-yellow-streaked grunts. And while I haven't seen any today, I've often spotted moray eels and groupers on this part of the reef.

In fact, the sheer number of species found on coral reefs is the most striking thing about this ecosystem. Efficient recycling can explain the reefs' high biomass, but it does not explain the great diversity of life. It is a problem that has long engaged ecologists. And though theories abound, none is widely accepted. According to E. O. Wilson, the Harvard biologist, "The cause of tropical preeminence [in biodiversity] poses one of the great theoretical problems of evolutionary biology."

Fortunately, we can try to understand and protect this ecosystem without solving the problem. It is clear that, in one way or another, virtually every organism found here depends on the reef. The corals provide shelter and food for a variety of invertebrates and fish, from sea stars to sea urchins, from butterfly fish to damselfish. More importantly, the reef provides a cultch to which sponges, sea fans, and many species of algae can attach themselves. These in turn provide food for everything from snails to parrotfish. The jumble of corals that makes up a reef also provides niches and crevices that harbor creatures as large as moray eels and as small as bacteria and filamentous algae. Clearly, the first step in protecting a reef ecosystem is to protect the corals.

Just before I reach the boat, I dive to get a closer look at a large, brown lump of boulder coral that rests on the sea floor among star corals and assorted gorgonians. Its surface is covered with thousands of small blisters, each of which is a coral polyp with its tentacles retracted. Come nightfall, when the zooplankton begin to rise, the blisters will open and tiny tentacles will unfurl and grab anything that comes within reach.

Some divers never get close enough to a coral head to see the tiny creatures that created it. To them, reefs appear monolithic, stable, and not in much need of protection. But appearances are deceiving. In truth, this ecosystem is balanced on a knife edge, and even small changes in the environment can produce disastrous effects.

Consider, for example, water temperature. Corals are found in waters with temperatures of sixty-four to ninety-seven degrees Fahrenheit, but they thrive only in seas where the mean temperature is between seventy-four and seventy-eight degrees, which is why reefs exist only in tropical waters. Unusually high or low temperatures can damage corals and sometimes kill them.

Corals are also sensitive to light, storms, predator irruptions, dynamite, anchors, cyanide, water salinity, sediments, and, most importantly, sea levels. Corals can survive only a few hours out of the water, so declining sea levels can turn a flourishing coral reef into a lifeless lump of limestone. The hills in the 13,500-acre Washington-Slagbaai National Park in the northeast corner of Bonaire are fossilized limestone terraces formed by living corals when sea levels were higher.

Rising sea levels usually—but not always—treat corals more kindly. Reef-building corals, like the boulder coral I inspected, are colonies composed of hundreds or thousands of polyps, each of which can divide by a process known as budding and produce another polyp. Each polyp creates and occupies its own calcium carbonate cup, called a corallite. However, part of the polyp protrudes above the lip of the cup and connects to its neighbors, creating a mat of living tissue that coats the surface of the coral colony. The mat is invisible because it is transparent, and it is covered with a thin film of mucus, which makes it sticky to the touch.

As the polyps, assisted by their resident algae, continue to secrete calcium carbonate, the coral skeleton grows upward and outward. To keep up, the polyps must periodically lay down a new base plate and move toward the surface. This is a painfully slow process. Still, it is fast enough to allow a reef to keep up with normal rises in sea level. But if the sea rises too rapidly, the reef can "drown." This occurs when the photosynthetic algae in the coral polyps get too little sunlight. The algae then become less productive and eventually die.

This is the beginning of the end of the reef. Although some deepwater corals survive without zooxanthellae, reef-building corals do not thrive without friendly algae to feed them and help them build their protective skeletons.

A rapid increase in sea levels would drive a stake through the heart of the world's reefs.

Kalli De Meyer is the tanned, youthful-looking manager of Bonaire Marine Park. She is a native of foggy London but seems quite at home on this sun-drenched island. Kalli has degrees in marine biology and oceanography and a clipped, businesslike British accent. She is aware that she runs one of North America's most successful sanctuaries, and she sometimes gives talks to representatives of other countries about how to establish and maintain marine parks.

Kalli knows she has inherited a dream sanctuary, an intact ecosystem that was protected before any significant damage was done to it. Because its rules were (and are) strict and rigorously enforced, the park has suffered little degradation in the years since it was established. The dynamite and cyanide fishing that has devastated many Pacific reefs has never been a problem here. And since the park funds itself by charging each diver a ten-dollar yearly admission fee, it is in no danger of becoming what Kalli calls a "paper park," a sanctuary that exists in name only, as is sometimes the case in the Caribbean.

"Education, research, and enforcement are what marine park management is all about," says Kalli. "No one comes to Bonaire to trash a reef. If damage is caused, it is most often through simple ignorance of the fragility of reef environments. And trying to run a marine park without research and monitoring is like trying to drive blindfolded." The third element—enforcement—should "kick in with the small percentage of users with whom education fails to make any impact."

Despite Kalli's efforts, the park faces threats. One is its ever-increasing popularity. When it was established in 1979, fewer than five thousand scuba divers used the park; by 1994, the number was up to twenty-five thousand and still growing. The park is, Kalli says, "approaching what we believe to be the carrying capacity of the reefs in terms of diver visitation." To combat this problem, she is trying to convince the local government to diversify Bonaire's tourist base.

Regardless of the outcome of her lobbying, the park faces other threats over which Kalli has little control. Sediment created by soil erosion from coastal-zone development can smother corals every bit as effectively as overgrown algae. Many marine biologists believe that this is the biggest problem facing reefs in the rapidly developing South Pacific—bigger even than dynamite and cyanide fishing. So far, though, sedimentation hasn't been a problem on Bonaire's reefs.

But even Bonaire could not escape coral bleaching, a widespread phenomenon that hit Caribbean and Pacific reefs in the 1980s and 1990s. Bleaching occurs when corals expel their zooxanthellae in response to an increase in water temperature or some other stress. Without their internal algae, the transparent corals appear white, the color of their limestone skeletons. And prolonged bleaching will eventually kill corals.

The tongue of warm water called El Niño has recently caused substantial bleaching of the Great Barrier Reef. Kalli says that when water temperatures on Bonaire's reefs exceed 85.1 degrees Fahrenheit, bleaching occurs. This has happened twice at the park, once in 1990 and again in 1995. However, few corals died, and I saw no aftereffects from bleaching when I was there in 1994 and 1997. No one knows for sure why Bonaire Marine Park escaped the devastating coral mortality that followed bleaching elsewhere in the Caribbean, but the immaculate condition of its reefs probably didn't hurt.

Perhaps the biggest problem the park faces is one that looms over every coral reef in the world: global warming. Since the Industrial Revolution, carbon dioxide in the atmosphere has increased from 280 to 360 parts per million. Carbon dioxide traps the sun's heat, and the Environmental Protection Agency reports that the earth's mean surface temperature rose about one degree Fahrenheit in the last century. In addition to causing bleaching, high water temperatures melt glaciers and other ice in the polar regions, which raises sea levels—four to ten inches in the last century alone.

In the coming century, sea levels are expected to rise even faster. Among the doomsday and the don't-worry numbers that swirl about this issue, the best estimate is probably the middle-of-the-road figure used by the EPA. It predicts that sea levels will rise thirteen inches in the next hundred years. The question that concerns the managers of the world's tropical marine parks is, Can reef-building corals keep up with this increase?

Some corals will have no problem. Staghorn coral, one of the major components of Bonaire's reefs, can grow up to 10 inches a year, fast enough to keep up with rising seas in all but the most catastrophic scenarios. But star coral, which is also important in Caribbean reefs, grows more slowly, only about 0.2 to 0.4 inch per year. Even so, that's 20 or more inches per century, a growth rate that should enable it to keep pace with rising sea levels.

Of course, all of this is guesswork. Nobody really knows how fast sea levels will rise, and nobody knows for sure how the reefs will react. And though a few scientists predict disaster, I'm betting on the reefs—and on Kalli De Meyer and the rest of us.

Sea levels have waxed and waned thousands of times since the first stromatolitic reefs rose in Precambrian waters, and stromatolites are still around today. The precursors of today's corals began building limestone reefs 500 million years ago. Since then, sea levels have fluctuated hundreds of feet, and reefs of one sort or another still exist. With that kind of record, it's possible to get complacent about the future of coral reefs.

Such complacency, however, would be misplaced. The fossil record shows that coral reefs have vanished from the earth several times, only to reappear a few million years later. Nobody knows what caused the demise of the reefs, but climate changes probably played a role. Which brings us back to Kalli De Meyer—and to the rest of us.

So far, Bonaire Marine Park's efforts to preserve the reefs—eliminating anchoring, stopping spearfishing and coral collecting, and instituting a don't-touch-the-reef policy—have been wildly successful, as has Kalli's emphasis on education, research, and enforcement. The remaining threats—sedimentation due to soil runoff, pollution, warming waters, and rising sea levels—are largely outside the park's control. And that's where the rest of us come in.

We must convince politicians to properly manage coastal-zone development; we must insist on adequate sewage treatment systems, and be willing to pay for them; and we must reduce the amount of carbon dioxide we spew into the air.

Sanctuaries are islands of hope surrounded by the rest of us. And ultimately, it is we who are responsible for their survival.

CHAPTER 2

*A*ncient Cypresses, Young Storks

Corkscrew Swamp Sanctuary, Florida

CORKSCREW SWAMP SANCTUARY lies just west of the Everglades, in southern Florida's Big Cypress Swamp. Ancient, never-cut cypresses tower over palms and pop ashes. Between canopy and shrubs is a bewildering profusion of exotic-looking epiphytes that cling to every surface. Herons and egrets stalk fish in the sanctuary's dark ponds, and in winter, the largest colony of wood storks in the United States nests here.

Although the sanctuary remains pristine, the land around it has changed dramatically in the last century. These changes have profoundly affected the wood storks. Behind their struggle to survive, and the sanctuary's struggle to help them, is a tale with a message that refuge managers everywhere are taking to heart.

The idea that changed the landscape of southern Florida came from an unlikely source, a well-to-do lawyer turned scholar named Thomas Buckingham Smith. Smith was born on Cumberland Island, Georgia, in 1810. While he was still a boy, his family moved to St. Augustine, Florida.

His parents were transplanted New Englanders, and his later life would prove that he absorbed some of their New England values.

After Buckingham's father was appointed United States consul to Mexico, the fourteen-year-old boy visited him there. During his visit, Buckingham Smith fell in love with the Spanish language and the history of Spanish-speaking people in North America. It was a romance that would last a lifetime.

Smith spent three years at Washington (later Trinity) College in Hartford, Connecticut, then moved on to Harvard Law School, graduating in 1836. After a stint in the law offices of a judge in Portland, Maine, he returned to St. Augustine to open his own law practice. And as many up-and-coming young lawyers do, he dabbled in local politics. This brought him to the attention of R. J. Walker, the secretary of the treasury of the United States.

Exactly what events led to the secretary's letter to Buckingham Smith on June 18, 1847, aren't clear, but the instructions contained in it were. The letter designated Smith an agent of the Treasury Department. It listed a few minor duties, then got to the point: "The most important service expected of you is the procurement of authentic information in relation to what are generally called the 'Everglades' on the peninsula of Florida." The idea behind the investigation was simple, even when phrased in nineteenth-century bureaucratese: "It has been represented to the department that there are several million acres of public lands in the vast lake called by that name [the Everglades] and which can be reclaimed and rendered valuable . . . [if] drained by two or three small canals." The Treasury Department wanted Buckingham Smith to determine if the Everglades could be drained.

A year later, Smith's report was on the secretary's desk. It started by naming the lakes and rivers within the Everglades and Big Cypress Swamp, which was also known as the Atseenahoofa. It spoke of elevations and geology, the contours of the land. The language was dry and technical. In the middle of the report, though, there was a surprise. As he began to describe the Everglades, his language became poetic, even romantic. Apparently, Buckingham Smith had fallen in love again. This time, the object of his affections wasn't Mexico, it was the Everglades.

> The appearance of the interior of the Everglades is unlike that of any region of which I have ever heard, and certainly it is in some respects the most remarkable on this continent.
> Imagine a vast lake of fresh water extending in every direction from shore to shore beyond the reach of human vision, ordinarily unruffled by a ripple on its surface, studded with thousands of islands of various sizes, from one-fourth of an acre to hundreds of acres in area and which are generally covered with dense thickets of shrubbery and vines. Occasionally an island is found with lofty pines and palmettos upon it, but oftener they are without any, and not unusually a solitary majestic palmetto is seen. . . . The water is pure and limpid and almost imperceptibly moves . . . silently and slowly to the southward. . . . The flexible grass bending gently to the breeze protects its waters from its influence. Lilies and other aquatic flowers of every variety and hue are to be seen on every side, in pleasant contrast with the pale green of the saw grass, and as you draw near an island the beauty of the scene is increased by the rich foliage and blooming flowers of the wild myrtle and honeysuckle and other shrubs and vines that generally adorn its shores. The profound and wild solitude of the place, the solemn silence that pervades it . . . add to awakened and excited curiosity feelings bordering on awe.

At that point in the report, the language changed again. The flinty New Englander replaced the romantic Spanish scholar, as Smith's practical sensibilities reasserted themselves. The change of tone wasn't surprising. Smith was a man of his time, and in those days, the wonders of nature played second fiddle to dominion and settlement.

> But if the visitor is a man of practical, utilitarian turn of thought, the first and abiding impression is the utter worthlessness to civilized

man, in its present condition, for any useful or practical object, of the entire region. A solitary inducement can not now be offered to a decent white man to settle in the interior of the Everglades.

Smith went on to say that draining the Everglades and the Atseenahoofa was eminently practical. He discussed the canals that would have to be dug, the rivers that would have to be deepened. He mentioned crops that could be grown on the drained land—"lemons, limes, oranges, bananas," and more. He attached letters from military men and engineers attesting to the practicality of his proposal. To those men, draining the Everglades and Big Cypress appeared to be a worthwhile undertaking—and one not too difficult.

Smith moved on to a distinguished career in the diplomatic service, with posts in Spain and Mexico. He also held public office in St. Augustine. But he was a staunch Unionist, a stance that forced him to leave home during the Civil War. He died during a visit to New York in 1871. He had a stroke while he was out for a walk. Unfortunately, the police thought he was drunk and tossed him in jail. The next morning, they transferred him to Bellevue Hospital, but it was too late. He died that same day.

In his will, he left bequests to several people, including some property to his ex-slave Jack. And as with his Everglades report, Buckingham Smith inserted a surprise. Near the end of the document, he reaffirmed his antislavery roots: "The rest and residue of my property . . . I give and bequeath to . . . the black people of St. Augustine & their successors in all time to come in such manner as she [the trust fund] shall choose to adopt . . . providing first for the aged and invalid."

At the time of his death, Buckingham Smith was a respected translator of historical Spanish documents (his best-known translation was *Narratives of the Career of Hernando de Soto*, published in 1866). He is best known today, however, for his report on the Everglades. Although he was clearly ambivalent about the region (as many Floridians still are), after weighing its beauty against its utility, he came down firmly on the side of utility. His report was the first serious proposal to drain southern Florida.

Although the hard work of taming the region wouldn't get under way for another fifty years, Buckingham Smith set the stage for the great drainage projects that followed. Those projects put the people of Florida on a collision course with the wildlife of the Everglades and Big Cypress Swamp. And one of the creatures most endangered by the projects was the wood stork.

The wood stork (*Mycteria americana*) is the only true stork to nest regularly in the United States. It is a long-legged, ungainly bird that stands about three and a half feet tall. Its plumage is white, except for the black feathers on the trailing edges of its wings and its short black tail. The wood stork's bill is long, massive, and slightly downcurved. Its head and neck are dark and unfeathered in the manner of some vultures, which suggests one of its many common names: flinthead. But its stately, hump-shouldered walk always reminds me of another nickname: preacher bird.

Wood storks nest across much of South America, but the largest nesting colonies in the pre-European United States were concentrated in the southern Florida wetlands, in the Everglades and Big Cypress Swamp. It was a landscape governed by the seasons, a cycle of wet and dry to which these birds were perfectly adapted.

The rains begin as spring ends. They come fitfully at first. Rainy afternoons are followed by days of sunny, humid weather. Occasional thunderstorms, short and violent, flash across the land. But this is only a warmup; the serious rains start in August. Dark clouds, gray and often tinged with violet, hang heavy over the Everglades. Inches of rain can fall in an hour, blurring the horizon, making land indistinguishable from sky.

Before the lake was diked and channeled, the rains filled Okeechobee, and the overflow spread southward on the peat and saw grass that overlies the region's flat limestone base. The result was a shallow sheet of water forty or so miles wide that flowed sluggishly toward Florida Bay. This watery expanse was made famous by Marjory Stoneman Douglas, who named it the "River of Grass."

To the west, in Big Cypress Swamp, the rains caused creek and swamp and lake to merge and form a shallow sea. When the rains finally stopped in late fall, the waters of Big Cypress and the Everglades began to recede. The water was concentrated in small ponds and sloughs that teemed with fish and frogs and gators. In that damp land of well-defined seasons, the wood stork flourished.

Fortunately, a few early naturalists recorded their observations of wood storks in southern Florida while the area was still close to its pre-European condition. And a good way to learn about these birds is to tag along with the naturalists as they venture into the swamps.

In *Life Histories of North American Marsh Birds*, the famous ornithologist Arthur Cleveland Bent described the wood storks' habitat, and the difficulties of reaching it:

> To see it [the wood stork] at its best one must penetrate . . . the big cypress swamps of Florida, where these stately trees tower for a hundred feet or more straight upward until their interlacing tops form a thick canopy of leaves above the dim cathedral aisles. One must work his way through almost impenetrable thickets of button willows, underbrush, and interlacing tangles of vines. He must wade waist deep or more in muddy pools where big alligators lurk unseen or leave their trails on muddy banks, as warnings to be cautious, or where the deadly moccasin may squirm away under foot or may lie in wait, coiled up on some fallen log, ready to strike. If not deterred by these drawbacks, or by the clouds of malarial mosquitos or by the hot, reeking atmosphere of the tropical swamps, he may catch a fleeting glimpse of the big white birds or hear their croaking notes as they fly from the tree tops above.

Some of the most detailed notes on wood storks were made by the great bird man himself, John James Audubon, during a trip through Florida in the 1830s (Proby 1974):

The Wood Ibis [wood stork] is rarely met with single, even after the breeding season, and it is more easy for a person to see an hundred together at any period of the year, than to meet with one by itself. Nay, I have seen flocks composed of several thousands, and that there is a natural necessity for their flocking together I shall explain to you. This species feeds entirely on fish and aquatic reptiles, of which it destroys an enormous quantity, in fact more than it eats. . . . To procure its food, the Wood Ibis walks through shallow muddy lakes or bayous in numbers. As soon as they have discovered a place abounding in fish, they dance as it were all through it, until the water becomes thick with the mud stirred from the bottom by their feet. The fishes, on rising to the surface, are instantly struck by the beaks of the Ibises, which, on being deprived of life, they turn over and so remain.

Another naturalist, Willard Eliot, described a nesting site in southern Florida in 1892 (Bent 1926):

Out in the center of the lake was a small island about 100 feet in diameter, with about 3 feet elevation above the water. There were several large cypress trees besides a thick undergrowth of bay trees. What a sight met our gaze from the shore, the trees on the island were white with the ibises standing close together on the limbs. . . . The ibises were nesting and we could see a number of the birds sitting on their nests. Most of the birds were on the island, but we found two trees near the shore, one had five nests and the other seven. After looking over the field I proceeded to climb the first tree, a large cypress, the nests were placed 50 feet from the ground and were saddled flatly on the top of a horizontal limb. One limb had four nests in a row and were so close together that their edges touched. A typical nest was 18 inches across by 5 inches deep outside, only slightly depressed inside, made of coarse sticks lined with moss and green bay leaves. The eggs were chalky white and nearly always blood stained; the average set is three but we found sets of two and four.

Later, in 1913, F. M. Phelps visited an active wood stork rookery in the Big Cypress region that held an estimated seven thousand nests (Bent 1926):

> Tree after tree bore from 12 to 20 or more nests of this species, and in one I counted 32. . . . At this season, the middle of March, nearly all the nests contained young.

The early naturalists got much of it right. As Audubon observed, wood storks are social birds. They feed in small flocks that coalesce into larger colonies in November or December, when they begin to nest in the cypresses of the Atseenahoofa or in the mangroves of the Everglades. They return to the same sites year after year. The males select likely looking trees and clack their heavy bills to attract females. This amateurish method of attracting a mate is necessary because wood storks lack syringeal muscles in their voice boxes, a requirement for producing the complex songs of more sophisticated sex seekers. About all storks can manage are decidedly unsexy croaks and hisses. After mating, each pair builds a nest in a tree that is on an island or over water. This helps protect its nestlings from terrestrial predators such as snakes and raccoons.

Although the early naturalists' accounts of wood storks' behavior were generally accurate, they missed one important point. None of them fully grasped the wood storks' feeding technique. And that seemingly minor point is key to understanding these birds.

Wood storks are grope feeders. They wade in shallow ponds with their bills in the water and their mandibles open. Whenever they feel something: *SNAP!* Audubon observed feeding wood storks. He said that, "when eating, the clacking of their mandibles may be heard at a distance of several hundred yards." But he thought they were driving fish to the surface and picking them off visually. Of course, Audubon didn't have access to an ornithological laboratory. But Philip Kahl did, and his experiments at the University of Georgia proved the grope-feeding theory. He reported his results in 1964 in a classic ornithological paper.

Kahl placed two captured storks in a wading pool filled with clear water and stocked with minnows. Even though the fish were in plain view, the storks invariably groped randomly for them, often in "empty" water. To further prove the point, he then partially blinded one stork by putting the halves of a blackened ping-pong ball over its eyes. The blinded bird was allowed to forage with its sighted companion. The result: "In every instance the partially blinded bird was as successful in capturing fish as the normal bird."

Why did wood storks become grope feeders? Possibly because their feeding ponds are often muddy and thick with vegetation. In such waters, sight feeding is virtually impossible. But there is another advantage to groping for food. If necessary, a hungry bird can hunt at night. This is important for wood storks because they need a prodigious amount of fish to survive.

Although you wouldn't guess it from watching preacher birds' deliberate movements, wood storks have an exceptionally high metabolism. Kahl estimated it at about one and a half times that of the average bird. When you combine wood storks' high metabolism with their large size (mature males weigh about six pounds), you get birds that eat a lot of fish—a little over a pound per day. In fact, wood storks are legendary trenchermen; one captive bird devoured over 650 one-inch fish in thirty-five minutes. With an appetite like that, the ability to feed at night might indeed be advantageous.

But grope feeding has its disadvantages, too. To find and capture fish blindly requires a high density of prey. A soaring osprey can locate the only fish in a lake and nail it, but a groping wood stork wouldn't have a chance of finding it.

Because wood storks and their chicks need a lot of fish concentrated in shallow pools, their habit of nesting in large colonies places stringent demands on their habitat. Kahl measured the length of a typical wood stork nesting cycle, from the first bill clacking to the departure of the last fledgling. He then calculated that a colony of six thousand pairs of wood storks (not an uncommon number at Corkscrew Swamp a few years back) would eat 2.5 million pounds of fish during the nesting season. As a consequence, nesting wood storks need highly productive wetlands to sustain them—wetlands such as those in the Everglades and Big Cypress Swamp, the same ones Buckingham Smith proposed to drain.

Over fifty years after Smith's report, only a few small tracts on the outskirts of the Everglades had been drained. The interior of southern Florida was still mostly wilderness, but its wildlife was already decimated. Plume hunters had slaughtered millions of birds, as well as one National Audubon Society warden, Guy Bradley, who tried to stop them. A steady stream of egret, tern, and heron feathers flowed from the Everglades to New York milliners, who created fashionable hats for fashionable ladies.

Birds weren't the only targets in the Everglades. One hunter claimed to have killed ten thousand alligators in one month near Shark River, in what is now Everglades National Park. He got fifty cents per hide, quite a haul for a month's work in those days. Despite the slaughter, the Everglades ecosystem, the River of Grass itself, remained essentially intact. But that five-thousand-year-old ecosystem, formed after the end of the last ice age, was about to be shattered. In 1904, the people of Florida elected Napoleon Bonaparte Broward as governor, and he pledged to implement Buckingham Smith's proposal.

Broward was forty-seven years old when he took office in 1905. He was a burly, muscular man over six feet tall. He came from Duval County in northern Florida, a member of a large, prominent family whose plantations and wealth had been wiped out in the Civil War. He had worked as a riverboat pilot, steamship captain, gun runner to Cuba, and sheriff of

Duval County. He was a populist who opposed railroad-company land grabs and who promised to drain the Everglades and use the proceeds from land sales to bolster the state's educational system.

Broward's plan to accomplish this was a simple one. He would dig canals to connect the Everglades to rivers that flowed east into the Atlantic Ocean. (A western canal connecting Lake Okeechobee to the Caloosahatchee River and the Gulf of Mexico was already in place.) Before the end of Broward's first year in office, two huge dredges, the *Everglades* and the *Okeechobee*, were ready to begin fulfilling his promise to the people of Florida.

In 1906, the dredges began digging the North and South New River Canals west of Fort Lauderdale. The going was slow, however, and when Broward left office three years later, only fifteen miles had been dug. Nevertheless, the governor was satisfied. His objective had been to "save and reclaim the people's land," and he was convinced that he had started an irreversible process to do that. Most of the people of Florida agreed with him. He became known as "the man who drained the Everglades," and when a new county was created around the growing hamlet of Fort Lauderdale, the state named it Broward County.

Broward was right about the irreversible process. In the coming years, armies of engineers transformed the Everglades. First, in response to the disastrous flood of 1928, which burst through a levee and killed nearly two thousand people, Hoover Dike was built around the southern shore of Lake Okeechobee. Then, in the mid-1950s, as part of a comprehensive water management project, the state began building levees in the Everglades themselves and setting aside 27 percent of the River of Grass for agriculture. Today, technicians control the water flow in the Everglades through an extensive network of canals and levees and water gates. Buckingham Smith's prediction that crops would thrive in the drained soil proved correct. Sugarcane and tomatoes now grow on what were formerly seasonal wetlands. And the great sheet of water that the winter sun once dried into ponds—concentrating fish in such numbers that even a grope feeder such as the wood stork could prosper—is gone.

To the west, in Big Cypress, the story was much the same—with one exception. Instead of saw grass, the region Buckingham Smith called the Atseenahoofa was spotted with stands of virgin cypresses, which were valuable as timber. Logging and draining for agriculture and development proceeded hand in hand. By 1954, about the time the great water management project was getting under way in the Everglades, only one significant strand of virgin bald cypresses remained. It was in Corkscrew Swamp, an area owned by two lumber companies and named for the twisting creek that flowed through it. In those cypresses nested most of the wood storks in the United States.

Because their feathers were unsuited for hats, wood storks survived plume hunting, but the loss of Corkscrew's rookery would devastate them. To the rescue came another Harvard graduate, John Hopkinson Baker, a man as much of his time as Buckingham Smith had been of his own. Fortunately, the times had changed.

———

Baker was, like Smith, a man with New England roots. He was a dedicated field birder and a member of the Nuttall Ornithological Club in his hometown of Cambridge, Massachusetts. After starting his career as a Wall Street investment banker, he became executive director of the Audubon Association (the predecessor of the National Audubon Society) in 1934, after ousting the association's president, T. Gilbert Pearson, in a bruising boardroom battle.

Baker brought to the job the know-how of a practical businessman and the streak of insensitivity that sometimes shows up in men who are used to being the boss. He told one warden who appeared at a board meeting proudly dressed in his Audubon uniform that he looked "like a policeman." Crushed, the man vowed that he would never wear the uniform again.

Nonetheless, Baker was an effective advocate for conservation. He was also familiar with southern Florida, where he had helped establish

Everglades National Park in 1947. Consequently, when he heard that the last strand of virgin trees in Big Cypress Swamp was about to be logged, he headed for Tampa.

He met with representatives of the landowners—the Lee Tidewater Cypress Company and Collier Enterprises—in March 1954. By year's end, the National Audubon Society, assisted by other conservation groups, had raised the money to buy 2,240 acres of the swamp. Surprisingly, the logging companies were sympathetic to Baker's effort and later chipped in more land at low cost. The result was the National Audubon Society's Corkscrew Swamp Sanctuary, a spectacular haven for ancient cypresses and nesting wood storks. Finally, it seemed, the preacher bird was safe. Unfortunately, the fate of a species is rarely that simple—and the wood stork was to prove no exception.

Corkscrew Swamp Sanctuary has grown into a 10,560-acre, picture-perfect natural area with a two-mile boardwalk that threads among five-hundred-year-old moss-draped cypresses that rise a hundred feet or more above the ground. I arrive at the sanctuary on a warm January morning with a soft blue sky overhead and follow the boardwalk into the green stillness of the swamp.

Ed Carlson, the sanctuary manager, says that his number-one priority is to "preserve the natural system," and he has obviously been successful in doing so. The swamp glows with health. The huge, buttressed trunks of bald cypresses, ringed by knees but needleless at this time of year, stand in ponds of clear, dark water. Plants and trees of every shade of green envelop the boardwalk. Egrets and herons prowl the shallows, and anhingas dry their wings in the brush. A red-shouldered hawk soars overhead.

I hurry along. I am looking for nesting wood storks, and I know exactly where to find them. But when I arrive at the spot, the cypresses are quiet and empty. When I stood here a few years ago, the trees were crowded with the coarse, oversized nests of hundreds of wood storks.

Waves of the great white birds were coming and going, regurgitating fish for their croaking, pleading chicks. Today, not a wood stork is to be seen.

I suspected that storks would be scarce. When I walked in on the boardwalk, high water covered ground that is usually dry this time of year. A wet winter means that the seasonal ponds that the wood storks depend on don't shrink, and the fish stay dispersed. With the fish scattered, grope feeders can't catch enough to feed a family, so the storks don't nest. This is a natural phenomenon; wood storks have always missed a nesting season every now and then when conditions weren't right. The trouble is, in southern Florida these days, they are refusing to nest more and more often. In fact, Corkscrew has had only one decent nesting season since 1992, and it was a pale imitation of the vintage years of the 1960s.

To find out why, I track down Shannon Ludwig, a wildlife biologist who works at the sanctuary.

We meet in a makeshift conference room that doubles as an entrance corridor to the sanctuary offices. Shannon is in his late twenties, a solid, muscular man of medium height with short brown hair. He is dressed in a faded gray T-shirt and jeans. He looks like a man who expects to sweat before the day is done.

He pulls up a chair across the table from me. I run through the questions I have prepared for him, questions that I hope will shed some light on the declining population of wood storks in Corkscrew.

"Are the hundred thousand or so visitors who pour through the sanctuary every year degrading the wood storks' nesting habitat?"

"Has water quality or quantity changed recently?"

"Has Corkscrew changed in some other way in the last fifty years?"

"Do you expect any wood storks to nest here this year?"

Shannon responds carefully to every question, but the answer to each of them is no. Visitors are confined to the boardwalk, he says, so they do little or no damage to the ecosystem. Water quality and quantity have remained essentially unchanged since the 1950s, when the first manager began keeping records. And as far as anyone can tell, the sanctuary looks almost exactly as it did when it was founded forty-five years earlier. On the last question, he hesitates before answering: "No, it's an unusually wet winter. The storks probably wouldn't nest here under any circumstances."

"If everything's the same," I say, "then what happened to the wood storks? Why have their numbers dropped even in normal, dry winters?"

Shannon begins slowly. "The wood storks that nest here feed in wetlands outside the sanctuary. The declining populations are a direct result of the loss of seasonally flooded wetlands in southern Florida—the wetlands associated with the shorter hydroperiods, not the deeper waters."

"Hydroperiod is the amount of time a wetland is wet?"

"Yes. Short-hydroperiod wetlands are higher and drier. They are also easier and cheaper to drain. Therefore, they are preferred by developers. When you lose those wetlands, you lose the early-season nesting capabilities of the storks. Historically, they started feeding in those areas early in the season—in November or December. That triggered their nesting instinct, and those areas are gone. Now, they have to wait until later to nest, after the deepwater wetlands shrink to the shallow ponds they need to feed in. So, if the rainy season starts early, they won't nest at all, and if they do, three or four days of hard rain will make the storks desert their nests."

Shannon winds up our session by handing me a bar graph of nesting stork populations in Corkscrew. The downward trend is obvious and seemingly inexorable, the annual count approaching zero. Suddenly, the wood storks' plight becomes clear to me. Buckingham Smith's legacy—the settlement of southern Florida—put the storks into direct competition with humans for the higher and drier land. Naturally, the wood storks are losing. But does that mean they are goners? That they will inevitably be extirpated in the United States?

When I get back to the motel, I pull out some papers on wood stork populations that I've been carrying around with me.

Counting wood storks is difficult. They are big birds, and as Arthur Cleveland Bent noted, they nest in rough country in large colonies. Consequently, most early naturalists didn't actually count them; they, well, guessed at their numbers. Over the years, those guesses have been steadily reduced by scientists. In the 1930s, one of the first estimates of nesting storks in the United States put their number at seventy-five thousand pairs. Later, that figure was revised downward to fifty thousand, then to thirty thousand. Following that, the Fish and Wildlife Service estimated that no more than fifteen thousand to twenty thousand pairs had ever nested in the United States, primarily in southern Florida.

Probably the best estimate, and certainly the most conservative, was made by Kushlan and Frohring, who in 1986 concluded that the number of wood storks in southern Florida never exceeded ten thousand pairs. Their data indicated that the birds' population in southern Florida had remained amazingly stable at around ten thousand pairs until 1967. Then the water management projects in the Everglades and the draining of Big Cypress Swamp caught up with them. As the foraging grounds shrank, stork populations in southern Florida plummeted. By 1982, they had declined 75 percent. This drop landed the storks on the endangered species list in 1984 and garnered them a million-dollar recovery plan aimed primarily at restoring their foraging habitat.

Since then, nesting wood storks have almost vanished from the Everglades and have declined at Corkscrew. Nevertheless, Linda Finger, the wildlife biologist at the Fish and Wildlife Service who monitors stork populations, says she is "quite optimistic" about their future. The wood storks, it seems, have developed their own recovery plan.

Prior to the 1960s, most wood storks nested in southern Florida but traveled widely after the breeding colonies dispersed. Wood storks have been reported as far north as southern Canada and as far west as Montana, and they are commonly seen in northern Florida, Georgia, and South Carolina. I once saw a flock of thirty or so storks soaring high above a marsh in coastal North Carolina. So what's a travel-savvy wood stork to do when its normal breeding ground can no longer support it? It appears that the answer is to breed farther north.

These days, wood storks are nesting regularly in the part of their range where they were once found only after the breeding season. The hegira north has helped; the number of nesting pairs has nearly doubled, from 4,073 in 1991 to 7,853 in 1995, when the last census was taken. During that period, the number of nesting pairs at Corkscrew fluctuated from a low of 300 to a high of 1,800, far below the normal range of 3,000 to 7,000.

This recovery has presented the folks who manage Corkscrew with a conundrum. Should they concentrate on maintaining the sanctuary in its present mint condition and forget about wood storks, the birds they once showcased? Or should they work to get the storks to return?

When I asked Shannon Ludwig this question, his answer was quick and to the point: "The storks may not need us as much as they used to, but we need them. When they return, we'll know this ecosystem is healthy."

The health of wildlife populations in all sanctuaries—regardless of size—depends on the larger world. Oil drilling menaces caribou migration routes in Arctic National Wildlife Refuge, one of North America's largest sanctuaries; lawsuits may reverse the wolf reintroduction at Yellowstone; and overfishing has destroyed the Georges Bank fishery, once one of the most productive ecosystems in the world.

This is old news to Ed Carlson, who has spent fifteen years at Corkscrew Swamp Sanctuary. His first priority is still to preserve the natural area entrusted to him, but his second is to educate the public about the sanctuary and the ecosystem that surrounds it.

Ed is a big man—tall, with some heft to him. He was educated as a zoologist at the University of South Florida in Tampa. When we meet in the sanctuary's "conference room," he is wearing the tan uniform of the National Audubon Society. He is an impressive figure, and I wonder if John Hopkinson Baker would have dared say that he looks "like a policeman."

The talk turns to storks and their declining presence at the sanctuary. I ask him about the changes that have reduced their foraging grounds.

"The biggest problems here in Collier County are housing developments and agriculture," Ed replies. "Over 90 percent of the county was once seasonally flooded. Thousands of acres have been drained for development and even more for conversion to citrus groves. The storks' nesting areas in the sanctuary are as pristine as ever, but to bring them back in their previous numbers, we must influence what goes on in the entire watershed. And we must convince the public that a healthy ecosystem is good for them, as well as for storks.

"Already in Collier County, we have water rationing during the dry season, because canals drain the water away before it can adequately recharge the aquifer. To make matters worse, the rivers get too much water in the wet season. After a heavy rain, farmers pump so much water out of their fields that it causes flooding downstream. More wetlands would allow the aquifer to recharge properly in the wet season, ameliorating both drought and flood.

"We must get this information out to the public; wetlands are good for wildlife *and* people."

To help accomplish that goal, the sanctuary has begun a capital campaign to raise funds for an education center. It also participates in a mitigation project aimed at restoring some of Big Cypress Swamp's lost wetlands. An ambitious wetlands restoration project is also being planned for the Everglades. If carried out, it would reverse Buckingham Smith's legacy and restore much of the River of Grass.

Sanctuary managers everywhere are agreeing with Ed. They have learned that protecting the lands for which they bear direct responsibility is no longer enough, that the boundaries that define those lands are merely lines on a map. They know that to protect their sanctuaries, they must reach out to the public and defend the ecosystem around them.

Probably no one ever stated this idea more clearly than John Donne: "No man is an *Iland*, intire of it selfe; every man is a peece of the *Continent*, a part of the *maine*." Although Donne was writing about people, his words apply to sanctuaries and the larger world that surrounds them. We may call them islands, but sanctuaries are not isolates; they are joined to the world.

CHAPTER 3

Where Butterflies Go

El Rosario Monarch Butterfly Preserve, Michoacán, Mexico

LAURA SNOOK HOPS OUT OF HER CANOE into the black, knee-deep water and pulls it over a beaver dam. Her short, brown hair bounces jauntily as she jumps back in and paddles to the side of the creek to wait. Somewhat less jauntily, I pull my own canoe over what seems like the fiftieth dam of the day. Although we met just this morning, I am getting used to following Laura's khaki shirt wherever it goes.

I cautiously lower myself into the canoe and resume paddling. The stream widens, and we finally reach open water. It is fall, and the cypresses in this eastern North Carolina swamp have turned bronze, forming a spectacular backdrop for the red maples, which glow pink and crimson in the late-afternoon sunlight. The reflection of the trees in the still water duplicates the riot of color above.

Laura points out rare aquatic plants, the purpose of our expedition. Parrot feathers here, liverworts there, and a half-dozen species of duckweed. She shows me cow lilies and water ferns, but she can't keep her eyes off the trees that surround the lake. "I'm a forester by training," she says with a smile, "and I love field work."

"Forester? You're a forester?"

She hands me a business card. Laura, it turns out, is Dr. Laura, assistant professor of conservation biology at Duke University.

"We need to talk," I say. "I've been trying to dig up some information about the oyamel forests in Mexico. I'm going down there in a couple of months."

"You're planning a trip to the butterfly preserves?"

"Yep. Monarchs winter in oyamel forests. Have you ever seen one?"

"Sure. I spent years working in the preserves."

"Whoever said it's better to be lucky than smart was right."

"What?"

"Never mind," I say, then ask the question I have been researching for weeks: "What are the prospects for the oyamel forests?"

Laura's smile vanishes. "Not good. The preserve system isn't working. Something has to be done."

To find out what has to be done, I have to go to the preserves. There, Laura promised, I will find monarch butterflies packed together in numbers so great it will boggle my mind.

How to get to the preserves? It's no piece of cake, so please pay attention. What follows was learned the hard way.

First, fly to Mexico City in January; then take a taxi to Terminal Poniente; catch a first-class bus to Zitáuaro; transfer to a second-class bus to Angangueo; check in at one of the town's two hotels (the bus stops at the Hotel Albergue Don Bruno); have a *cerveza* or two; and ask for Alejandro Castro. When he arrives, say "El Rosario," followed by *"Cuánto?"* Watch a beatific smile light up his boyish face, listen to some really rapid Spanish, then pass him a piece of paper and a pencil. After he writes "200 pesos" (about $25) on the paper, say *"Sí"* and watch as he runs down the stairs laughing, pumping his fists in the air, yelling "Yes! Yes! Yes!" Do all of those things and you will be ready to visit one of North America's most important and endangered wildlife sanctuaries.

Alejandro meets me the next morning in front of the hotel. I slide into the front seat of a Ford pickup. Alejandro—who appears a bit young to have a driver's license—looks serious this morning, and his father, who leans against the wall of the hotel watching carefully, looks equally serious. We bump down a cobblestone street. Alejandro drives slowly, both hands on the steering wheel.

The road climbs away from Angangueo—a remote mountain village of about three thousand *gente* located seventy-five miles west of Mexico City—and changes from pavement to dirt to deeply rutted clay. The village sits about eight thousand feet above sea level, and the cool morning gets cooler as we climb. The land along the road is steeply sloped and terraced with rank upon rank of cornfields with last year's stubble still visible. Dark evergreens border occasional meadows, golden at this time of year with hay and haystacks. Small houses painted pink or green or brown cling to the sides of the mountains. The road is so rough and steep that Alejandro has to slow down to five miles an hour.

Suddenly, three campesinos materialize out of the morning mist. One of them tugs on something at the base of a tree. A thick chain rises from the roadbed and bars our path. One of the campesinos walks toward the car. He has dark, Indian-like features and wears a worn wool serape. He looks like a bandito from *Treasure of the Sierra Madre*. He is not smiling.

Alejandro rolls down his window. He is not smiling either. They talk in Spanish, voices low and tense. Finally, Alejandro fumbles in his pocket and extracts a few pesos. Money changes hands, the chain is dropped, and we continue toward El Rosario. Alejandro smiles expansively and launches into an excited monologue of which I understand not a word. Moments later, we pull into a parking lot crowded with vendors selling everything from tortillas to T-shirts. Alejandro yawns, buys a tortilla from a woman who is grilling them over a wood fire, and points out the path that leads to El Rosario. I begin to climb toward the preserve.

By the time I reach the small visitor center at the preserve's entrance,

I am panting. Since leaving Mexico City, I have done nothing but climb, and now, on foot, the altitude has taken the spring out of my step. I pay twelve pesos at the entrance and follow a long-legged guide up a well-tended path. The trail is bordered by a rickety wooden fence. On the other side, a boy herds some just-shorn sheep across a meadow. Beside the path lies the faded orange wing of a monarch butterfly. I pass another wing and then another.

The path continues to climb; I continue to pant; the number of butterfly wings beside the trail continues to grow. This place seems more like a monarch butterfly graveyard than a preserve. I pass a sign that gives the altitude: 3,100 meters. Over 10,000 feet, I calculate, and I have yet to see a live butterfly. I loiter along the trail, and my guide vanishes into the distance.

Up here, there is no fence, and what I take to be the preserve's boundary is marked by only a thin veil of trees. In an adjacent field, a farmer is plowing up last year's corn crop. His tractor is a mule with a graying muzzle. Light frost covers the ground. A dead monarch falls from a tree, spiraling gracefully to the ground. I examine it; much of its abdomen is missing.

Suddenly, the forest vanishes. The trail enters a blessedly level plateau covered with grass and small bushes and speckled with orange butterflies. For the first time, I know I've come to the right place. These monarchs are immobile, but they aren't dead. An occasional shiver of an outspread wing gives them away. Out here, in the open, the sun feels almost hot, and I suspect that the monarchs are warming themselves. One takes off from the grass and flies around for a moment, then lands in a bush. As I watch, more butterflies flutter into the air. I stand entranced for five minutes. There are more monarchs on this one patch of ground than I have seen in my entire life.

After the brief level interlude, the path resumes its steady climb and enters a wooded grove dominated by dark firs. They are oyamels (*Abies religiosa*), the trees these monarchs prefer for their winter roosts. A few butterflies flit through the quiet, still woods, which seem otherwise unin-habited. Gradually, my eyes make out great gray globs hanging from the lower branches of the oyamels. This is the real thing—the wintering site of millions of monarch butterflies. They are clinging to the firs with their wings up, showing only the drab undersides. I sit down on a nearby rock to take them in.

Groups of people, escorted by the guides who accompany all visitors to the preserve, come and go. Most of the visitors ooh and aah for a moment, then begin the trek back. Perhaps because I look harmless and can't understand a word they say, the guides allow me to sit unattended on my rock. And as I sit, the forest around me changes.

The gray globs on the firs slowly turn to orange as the monarchs open their wings to absorb sunlight. As they warm up, more and more of them take to the air. Soon, the woods are full of butterflies, a swirling, dazzling kaleidoscope of bright orange flickers among the somber firs.

The monarchs fly only a short distance, then land on rocks, on bushes, and on my head. The path itself turns orange as thousands of butterflies light on it. So thick are they that the guides rope off the upper part of the trail to prevent visitors from stepping on the groggy creatures.

How many monarchs are here? I have no idea. One entomologist estimated that over 100 million of them winter in these mountains. Cer-tainly, at this one site, they number in the millions. One slightly tattered monarch lights on the back of my hand and sips salty sweat. Could I have seen this same butterfly back home in North Carolina? Could this fragile creature have flown thousands of miles? Over the years, many lepi-dopterists have asked themselves that question, and it is only recently that they have learned the answer.

The monarch (*Danaus plexippus*) is a large orange-and-black butterfly. Its caterpillar is equally colorful, having a stubby body ringed with bands of black, white, and yellow. During summer, both forms of this showy insect can be found from southern Canada to northern Texas.

Because monarchs are large and common, naturalists have paid a lot of attention to them. Lincoln Brower, the world's foremost expert on monarchs, summarized the work of early naturalists in a 1995 paper for the *Journal of the Lepidopterists' Society*. He cited observations going back to 1857, when W. S. M. D'Urban wrote that the butterflies could be found in the Mississippi Valley in "such vast numbers as to darken the air by the clouds of them."

As nineteenth-century naturalists learned more about these butterflies, they zeroed in on a key question: What happens to monarchs when they disappear during the winter? Most naturalists assumed that monarchs survived cold weather by moving to the southern part of their range and hibernating in sheltered nooks such as hollow trees and rotting logs.

Then, before the turn of the century, colonies of wintering monarchs were found on California's Monterey Peninsula, clinging in dense clusters to pines and eucalyptus trees. Shortly thereafter, naturalists established that there were two populations of the butterflies. Those monarchs west of the Rockies migrated south and west and wintered in coastal California, roughly from San Francisco to Los Angeles. After this discovery, migration replaced hibernation as the most likely theory to explain the winter disappearance of the much larger population of eastern monarchs. But their wintering grounds remained a mystery.

And so things stood until 1975, when Kenneth and Cathy Brugger, associates of Canadian entomologist Fred Urquhart, discovered the site.

Entomologists tend to be obsessed. Take, for example, the greatest bug man of all, French entomologist Jean Henri Fabre (1823–1915). Fabre was a recluse in his village, preferring the company of insects to that of humans. He often addressed his closest friends in his writings: "Come here, one and all of you—you, the sting bearers, and you, the wing-cased armour-clads—take up my defence and bear witness in my favour." But obsession has its rewards. Near the end of his life, Fabre was acclaimed as one of the world's most important scientists, and the village he shunned erected a statue in his honor.

Following in Fabre's footsteps, Fred Urquhart became obsessed with monarch butterflies. In the preface to his book *The Monarch Butterfly: International Traveler*, he gave readers a brief autobiography. Urquhart was born in Toronto, Canada, in 1911. Even as a child, insects fascinated him, and by the time he was eight, he was collecting them. When he was sixteen, a biology teacher showed him some mounted specimens of monarch butterflies. It was the beginning of a lifelong love affair.

After college, Urquhart became curator of insects at the Royal Ontario Museum. By 1937, he was trying to figure out where monarchs spent the winter. All that was known of the eastern migration was that the butterflies headed south in late summer. Following them on foot was out of the question. Monarchs can cruise eighty miles a day when migrating. Cars were also useless, since monarchs don't stick to the roads.

Finally, Urquhart decided that the best way to track monarchs as they moved south was to tag them, but tagging butterflies turned out to be trickier than expected. Despite their wingspan of nearly four inches, monarchs are lightweights, weighing about one-fiftieth of an ounce. Metal tags, therefore, were too heavy. Glued-on paper tags proved to be messy and sticky and hindered the butterflies' flight. Gummed labels washed off in the rain. Urquhart finally settled on tiny, pressure-sensitive labels similar to those used as price tags. On them, he printed the words *Send to Zoology University Toronto Canada*. Then he appealed for volunteer taggers.

Over the years, thousands of monarchs were tagged, and hundreds of tags were returned to Urquhart. Gradually, a pattern revealed itself; most of the eastern monarchs were migrating in a diagonal path across the United States, from northeast to southwest, and wintering somewhere in southern Texas or northern Mexico. Urquhart and his wife, Norah, spent the winter of 1969–70 at the University of Texas at Kingsville, driving thousands of miles from their base to look for monarchs. The expedition failed; during the entire winter, they saw only two monarch butterflies. More than likely, the butterflies wintered farther south, Urquhart concluded.

Fortunately, one of his volunteers, an engineer named Kenneth Brugger, lived in Mexico City. Brugger and his wife, Cathy, who was Mexican, took up the cause, cruising the back roads of central Mexico in a motor home. After almost two years of searching, they located the wintering grounds of the monarch with the help of local woodcutters. Urquhart told the story in a 1976 article for *National Geographic*. "On the evening of January 9, 1975," he wrote, "Ken telephoned us from Mexico. 'We have located the colony,' he said, unable to control the excitement in his voice. 'We have found them—millions of monarchs—in evergreens beside a mountain clearing.'"

Amazingly, when the Urquharts visited the site a year later, Fred plucked from a mass of monarchs a butterfly bearing one of his tags. It had been attached in Chaska, Minnesota. As Fabre's obsession had paid off, so had Fred Urquhart's. But though the migration route of eastern monarchs was established, many questions remained unanswered. For example, why do monarchs—almost alone among insects—migrate at all? What makes a frail insect weighing a fraction of an ounce fly thousands of miles? The answer, it turns out, is an unassuming plant called milkweed.

Milkweeds belong to the family Asclepiadacae, a widespread group of plants. Over a hundred members of this family are found in North America alone. The most abundant species in eastern North America is common milkweed (*Asclepias syriaca*), which grows in abandoned fields and along roadsides from southeastern Canada to Georgia. It is a tall plant, nearly six feet in height, with pink flowers and a seed pod that splits open to reveal a ball of silky hairs similar to that of a dandelion. Although milkweed floss was once used as a replacement for kapok in life preservers and Thomas Edison thought its milky sap might be used to manufacture rubber, the plant is considered by most people to be, well, a weed.

Farmers and ranchers are especially averse to milkweed; they believe it is poisonous to livestock. Most guides to poisonous plants confirm this. One states unambiguously that milkweed is "extremely poisonous to humans and livestock." (Fred Urquhart noticed that cattle in Florida and on some Caribbean islands avoided eating milkweed as they grazed.) Other guides point out that milkweed may be merely distasteful to animals and that no human deaths have ever been reported from eating the plant. In fact, preparations of milkweed have long been used in folk medicine to cure everything from dropsy to asthma, and the name *Asclepias* comes from the Greek god of healing. Nonetheless, there is no doubt that milkweed contains harmful chemicals.

Because plants can't run from enemies, they have become specialists in biological warfare, manufacturing an array of noxious chemicals to ward off animals that would eat them. Milkweed's specialties are cardiac glycosides (often called cardenolides), complex organic molecules related to digitalis, which is used to treat heart disease. Most scientists believe these cardenolides give milkweed its bitter taste and make it unpalatable or even poisonous to animals.

One exception is the monarch. Although the adult butterflies live exclusively on nectar, monarch caterpillars adore milkweed leaves. In fact, having evolved a tolerance for cardenolides, they will eat nothing but milkweed. Early naturalists reported that monarch caterpillars also ate bitterroot, a member of the dogbane family, which is closely related to milkweed. So persistent were these reports that Susan Borkin, a scientist at a Milwaukee museum, decided to test the caterpillars' dietary preferences. She collected monarch caterpillars and placed them in plastic bags with leaves of either bitterroot or milkweed. In every case, the caterpillars died (presumably from starvation) before they would eat bitterroot. Meanwhile, the control caterpillars munched away happily on milkweed leaves.

Milkweed cardenolides are passed from caterpillar to butterfly, making both forms of the insect distasteful to some predators. But the taste is apparently not bad enough to deter the truly hungry. Birds and mice are known to prey on wintering monarchs, and the butterfly wings I saw on the path at El Rosario were probably the remains of grosbeaks' meals.

To accommodate their offspring's restrictive diet, monarch mothers lay their minuscule, ivory-colored eggs on milkweed leaves. After hatching, the larvae immediately begin eating the leaves on which they were born.

It was the search for milkweed that led the monarchs north. Most (but not all) scientists believe that monarchs, or their progenitors, learned to love milkweed in the South American tropics. So they were already hooked on the plant when they crossed the land bridge into Central America about three million years ago. The North American prairies, rich in milkweed, were expanding at the time, and the monarchs continued north to make use of that vast supply of caterpillar food. Although milkweed flourished in the cooler northern climate, the butterflies' tropical origins meant they had to retreat south during the winter to avoid freezing to death.

Thus was born the migratory pattern of modern monarchs. But understanding the pattern turned out to be the easy part of the problem; figuring out how the monarchs actually accomplish their migration is the hard part.

After the Bruggers' discovery in 1975, scientists located other wintering sites. According to Stephen Malcolm, a monarch researcher from Western Michigan University, "Hundreds of millions of butterflies east of the Rocky Mountains and Great Plains coalesce into 10 sites near the center of Mexico." The individual sites are small, ranging in size from less than an acre to eight acres. Every site is in an oyamel forest at an altitude of about ten thousand feet in the Transverse Neovolcanic Belt— a range of east-west mountains that bisects central Mexico. All of the sites lie along a sixty-mile arc that runs northwest from Nevada de Toluca in the state of México to Contepec in Michoacán.

Monarchs begin moving out of their wintering sites in late March. The butterflies fly north—feeding, mating, and laying eggs on newly emerged milkweed along the Gulf Coast from Texas to Florida. Then they die. The next generation continues in a generally northeasterly direction toward the Great Lakes and southern Canada, except for a small population that heads due north into the Plains states.

Several generations later (the number of monarch generations varies from three to five per year), the monarchs stop reproducing and begin assembling in colonies that move south, flying only during the daylight hours, spending the nights clustered on trees along their route. Somehow, these monarchs, none of which has ever been to Mexico, find their way back to the same few wintering areas that their forebears left months ago.

Lincoln Brower has suggested that the monarchs navigate by orienting themselves to the earth's magnetic field, but no one has explained how they wind up in the same tiny areas year after year. However they manage it, the butterflies' remarkable migration is clearly not something learned; it is hard-wired behavior.

Exactly when eastern monarchs began wintering in oyamel fir forests is not clear. We know today that these forests fit the needs of the species perfectly. Summer monarchs live only a few weeks; males die shortly after mating, and females die after laying their eggs. The winter generation of North American monarchs, however—those that roost in Mexico or along the California coast—live for half a year or longer. These butterflies spend much of the winter in a dormant state and postpone mating until spring. The monarchs I encountered in El Rosario were so sluggish that visitors inadvertently stepped on them. This could never happen to fast-flying summer monarchs. Dormancy and celibacy allow the winter generation to live longer than the butterflies of summer.

To become dormant, monarchs need cool weather. The cooler it is, the more dormant they become. If it warms up, as it did when I was at the refuge, the butterflies become active and can fritter away the energy they need for spring migration and mating. Of course, if it gets too cold, they freeze. But monarchs can survive temperatures only slightly below freezing, so disaster lies just a few degrees on either side of thirty-two degrees Fahrenheit. The oyamel forests of Mexico's Transverse Neovolcanic Belt offer this narrow band of temperatures.

But proper ambient air temperature isn't the only condition necessary for the butterflies' survival. As Lincoln Brower has pointed out, rainfall can freeze monarchs at temperatures they would otherwise survive, but too little moisture can desiccate them, with equally calamitous results. Radiant cooling, caused by exposure to the clear night sky, can also reduce the butterflies' temperature and kill them. And in some years, unusually severe snowstorms knock millions of monarchs from their protective firs and bury them in snow, where they usually die.

In truth, wintering monarchs live on the edge of catastrophe, and without the stable climate of the oyamel forests, few would survive the winter. And those forests are vanishing.

People and climate change pose the biggest threats to Mexico's oyamel forests. Oyamels—like most firs—are boreal trees. The Mexican fir forests formed during the glacial periods of the Pleistocene (1.8 million to 10,000 years ago), when cool weather encouraged northern trees to spread south. When the climate began warming at the end of the Pleistocene, heat-tolerant pines and oaks began displacing the oyamels. The oyamel forests retreated to higher elevations. Today, only about a hundred thousand acres of these forests survive in Mexico. They are confined to the mountains, where they hang on as dark green islands at elevations between eight thousand and twelve thousand feet. And as the climate continues to warm, the forests will continue to shrink.

However, the campesinos living near these remnant forests pose a more immediate threat. Although they have lived side by side with the butterflies for centuries, population growth has spurred them to increase their logging of the forests. Because wintering monarchs are concentrated in just a few sites, the eastern population is extremely vulnerable to changes in those areas.

Convinced of the importance of those sites to wintering monarchs, President Miguel de la Madrid signed a decree in 1986 to protect five of the most important ones. Altogether, the decree gave limited protection to nearly forty thousand acres of oyamel forests. Each site was divided into a core zone, in which all logging and farming was to be prohibited, and a buffer zone, in which those activities were to be banned only when butterflies were present. It was a great victory for conservation—except for a few details. And as usual, the devil was in the details.

It appears that protecting wintering monarchs would be a simple task. Their locations are known and discrete and occupy a relatively small area. Also, monarchs are charismatic creatures with a group of enthusiastic followers. But protecting the sites has turned out to be anything but easy.

The problems that hinder today's conservationists have their roots in the bloody soil of 1917. In that year, following a long and terrible revolution, Mexico adopted a new constitution. One part of the constitution was an agrarian reform plan, outlined in the famous Article 27. Historian T. R. Fehrenbach described it this way: "The heart of Article 27 was the assertion that all soil belonged to the sovereignty, which might grant or revoke it according to the national need. This was a return to Hispanic medievalism that would permit the expropriation of both haciendas and oil fields." The government also agreed to make land available to agrarian collectives, known as *ejidos*.

In the 1930s alone, the Mexican government expropriated 45 million acres, mostly from large landowners, and distributed it to individual families and *ejidos*. Almost all of the land on which the butterflies winter is *ejido* land. And when the government used its sovereign rights to protect those properties—as it could do under Article 27—it neglected to pay the *ejidatarios* for the loss of their land. Thus, the people who had felled trees on those lands for years—for fuel, to build houses, to clear land for farming, and to sell—found their rights taken away without a peso in recompense. Furthermore, Article 27, which made land available to the *ejidos*, gave the *ejidatarios* only the right to work the land but not to sell or rent it. This Catch-22 has prevented environmental groups from buying the land and establishing private sanctuaries.

Quite naturally, the *ejidatarios* are not happy about the preserves. The butterflies don't merely inconvenience them; they cost them income. Because subsistence farmers, in Mexico as elsewhere, live on the brink of poverty, any loss of income is serious business. Consequently, some *ejidatarios* ignore the proscription against logging and take an oyamel tree when they need one. This practice thins the forest and opens the canopy, which destroys the umbrella that shields the butterflies from rain and snow and the cold night sky. An open canopy also insolates the monarchs during the day, which rouses them from their protective torpor.

It is these practices that made Laura Snook, who worked among the *ejidatarios*, pessimistic about the future of the monarch preserves.

"Education, research, and enforcement" are the keys to managing a successful sanctuary, said Kalli De Meyer of Bonaire Marine Park. In the present case, lax enforcement of the 1986 presidential decree is part of the problem, but it is clear that the ills afflicting the monarch preserves lie deeper than that.

The boundaries of the preserves are not clearly marked. This encourages poaching of trees, because ambiguity makes it easy to fool yourself about which side of a line a tree is on. It is especially easy to fool yourself if you are an *ejidatario* who wants the wood to cook tortillas or to sell for a few pesos so you can join the well-heeled tourists in Angangueo for a *cerveza* or two. And since this land was open to logging until the government put it off-limits, it is easy to rationalize your behavior. So rigorous enforcement might slow the poaching, but it won't stop it until the *ejidatarios* are satisfied they are no longer getting the short end of the stick. But if the preserves could be shown to help them rather than harm them, they might adopt a more positive attitude.

Showing the *ejidos* how to profit from the preserves was the task undertaken by Monarca, A.C., a Mexican environmental organization that was active in the 1980s and early 1990s but is now dormant for lack of funds. And this approach is working—albeit in a limited way.

The problem is this: Of the five preserves established by the 1986 decree, only two are open to the public, and of the two, only El Rosario is easily accessible to tourists. The rights to the lands protected by the decree belong to thirty or more *ejidos*, but the land on which El Rosario sits belongs to only one. Consequently, it is the only *ejido* that profits much from the tourist trade.

The men who stopped us on the road to the preserve, the vendors selling tortillas and soft drinks in the parking lot, the guides at the preserve, and the folks running the visitor center belong to that *ejido*. And its members do make some well-deserved pesos from ecotourism during the four or five months that the monarchs are there. But the other *ejidos* get nothing, which doesn't sit well with their disgruntled members. And as we saw in Corkscrew Swamp Sanctuary, even the best-run preserves need good neighbors.

With the oyamel forests in trouble, what are the prospects for eastern monarchs? Well, it's unlikely that the butterflies will change their ways. Their migratory patterns and whatever it is that guides them back to their wintering sites are clearly instinctual. Therefore, to protect the eastern monarchs, those sites must be preserved. Opinions on whether or not that will happen vary with whom you ask.

Laura Snook, who has spent a lot of time at the sites, is mostly gloomy. "Forest continues to be lost, and the butterflies' habitat is deteriorating," she says. "A strategy needs to be developed to compensate the *ejidos* for the timber they are cutting from the preserves. Otherwise, they will continue to poach. If we fail to do that, the forest will continue to decline as long as the *ejidatarios* continue their subsistence way of life. There is some hope, though. Young people are leaving the villages, and emigration may take some of the pressure off the forests."

Lincoln Brower is slightly more upbeat: "The main problem is the preserves are being whittled away. The only enforcement is near the butterflies. Which means the ecosystem itself is not being protected. The Mexican government is aware of this. They want to expand the boundaries of the preserves. This is a good idea, but if enforcement is not improved, it may not work out any better than the current system."

The most optimistic expert of all is Susana de Castilla, who worked for Monarca, A.C.: "The community is improving with the increased organization of public access to the sanctuary. And most importantly, the monarch butterfly will continue to visit its oyamel fir overwintering forest each winter for the foreseeable future."

Clearly, several things must be done to safeguard the monarchs' wintering sites. First, protection should be extended to all of the sites, not just the current five. Second, the *ejidatarios* must be compensated for their loss of land. Third, ecotourism should be encouraged and managed in ways that benefit both the butterflies and the *ejidos*.

And progress is being made on at least one front. A budding ecotourism business is taking hold in Angangueo. With toll collectors that look like banditos and ebullient entrepreneurs like Alejandro Castro, there is hope—for people and butterflies.

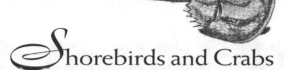

$\mathscr{S}$horebirds and Crabs
Cape May National Wildlife Refuge, New Jersey

I FOLLOW KIMBLES BEACH ROAD until it dead-ends at Delaware Bay. Friends have told me that this section of the eighty-three-hundred-acre Cape May National Wildlife Refuge offers the best birding, and one glance is enough to tell me why. The tide is high, and the narrow strip of sand above the wrack line is carpeted with thousands of birds, so thick in places that they obscure the beach.

Most conspicuous are the laughing gulls, quarrelsome, black-headed loudmouths. They are surrounded by the russets, grays, and browns of the smaller and far more numerous shorebirds. The shorebirds—ruddy turnstones, semipalmated sandpipers, sanderlings, and red knots—stand quietly, preening and resting. Beyond them, horseshoe crabs crawl through the muddy shallows of the bay, and the gulls peck viciously at a few that were upended by the light surf and stranded upside down on the shore. Occasionally, a group of laughing gulls takes to the air, and their raucous cries ring out over the water.

Both birds and crabs look very much at home in this primeval panorama. But in fact, they are short-term visitors to these shores, as temporary as the tourists who stroll the sidewalks and beaches of the old resort town of Cape May, New Jersey, ten miles to the south. Unlike the tourists, though, their presence here on a cool, cloudless spring afternoon is a matter of life and death. Regrettably, the scene in which they are participants is a threatened phenomenon, and the problem facing crabs and birds is as old as mankind itself—the overharvesting of a critical resource.

Most of the shorebirds that frequent Cape May in the spring are long-distance migrants, but even among those hardy travelers, red knots (*Calidris canutus*) stand out. Although a few sensible knots winter in Florida, most of those on the beach at Cape May started their journey in Argentina, some as far south as Tierra del Fuego.

And they won't be here long. In a week or two, they will resume their northward flight, finally winding up on their breeding ground north of Hudson Bay in Canada's Northwest Territories. After a few months in the Arctic, the knots will reverse course and head south for Argentina. It is a restless, exhausting life, one that seems especially unsuitable for a dumpy ten-inch-long bird.

Red knots get their common name from their pale red breasts and their cries, which sound like "knut." Their scientific name, bestowed upon them by Linnaeus himself, comes from the Greek *kalidris*, meaning "water bird," and from King Canute, the monarch of Norway, Denmark, and England. Why the great Swedish naturalist chose the epithet *canutus* is not known; Canute was a Dane, and it may have been simply to honor a fellow Scandinavian. But the king was a much-traveled Viking, and Linnaeus may have had that in mind when he named the species. If so, he hit the nail on the head.

Red knots migrate up to eighteen thousand miles a year, only a few thousand miles less than a pole-to-pole round trip. If a knot managed to reach age thirteen (not an impossibility), it would have flown a distance in its annual migrations equal to a trip to the moon. And like space travelers, knots do their flying in long, nonstop stretches. Brian Harrington, the ornithologist at Manomet Bird Observatory in Massachusetts who pieced together the migration routes of North American red knots, believes that some southward-bound knots fly nonstop from New Jersey to South America, covering five thousand miles in less than six days. Knots, like other shorebirds, expend enormous amounts of energy on those marathon flights, and when they land, they are lean and hungry.

By the time a red knot arrives at Delaware Bay, it has burned up all of the fat (and often some of the muscle) it had accumulated during its wintering season in South America. To continue its flight to the Arctic breeding grounds, it must put on a lot of weight in a hurry. Now, one hungry bird can easily find enough food to prepare itself for such a flight, but knots travel in flocks, and they arrive at the bay at the same time as other migratory shorebirds. In 1982, celebrated birder Pete Dunne and his associates counted 420,000 shorebirds in one day along a hundred-mile stretch of Delaware Bay shoreline. And biologist Joanna Burger has estimated that over 1,000,000 shorebirds pass through Delaware Bay each spring, which is about 80 percent of the entire shorebird population of eastern North America. When those 1,000,000 hungry birds descend on the bay, they need a lot of food, and the delicacy they prefer is horseshoe crab eggs.

In early spring, as a red knot fattens itself in Argentina in preparation for its flight north, a female horseshoe crab's biological alarm clock rings, announcing that the spawning season is near. She emerges sluggishly from the mud where she has spent the winter and begins a journey to the shores of Delaware Bay, as her forbears did for millennia before her.

Along with the coelacanth and the cockroach, the horseshoe crab (*Limulus polyphemus*) has long been tagged with the oxymoron *living fossil*. This means that scientists have found fossilized creatures in ancient rocks that closely resemble today's horseshoe crabs. Paleontologists have traced the lineage of horseshoe crabs back to the sea scorpions that lived from

230 to 425 million years ago; crabs of the genus *Limulus* appeared in the fossil record about 200 million years ago. Those fossilized crabs bear an uncanny resemblance to the horseshoe crabs of our time. That kind of longevity has attracted the attention of scientists, who would like to know the species' secrets of success. Their research has shown that horseshoe crabs have unusual features found in no other living animals.

Four species of horseshoe crabs exist today, but only one of them, *L. polyphemus*, is found in North America. Horseshoe crabs consist of three parts, which are hinged together. The largest segment is the forepart, a broad, brown carapace (technically a prosoma) shaped like a horse's hoof. So obvious is this resemblance that early North American settlers called them "horsefoot crabs," a name that changed over the years to "horseshoe." To the large carapace is attached a smaller, spine-edged carapace, which is in turn attached to a long, sharp-tipped tail, or telson. Altogether, a large female *Limulus* can weigh up to ten pounds and reach a length of two feet and a width of half that. And after your first look at one, you may rightly guess that there's nothing else like it in the world.

The physiology of the horseshoe crab is even stranger than its appearance. Take, for example, the eyes: there are nine of them, two pairs on each side of the large carapace and five vestigial eyes below it. Or the jaws: it has none and uses its five pairs of legs to masticate its food. Or the blood: it is copper based, turns blue on exposure to air, and is exceptionally resistant to bacterial infections. Or even the name: horseshoe crabs aren't crabs at all; they belong to the class Merostomata, a group more closely related to spiders than crabs.

But it isn't these oddball characteristics that bring the shorebirds to Delaware Bay; it is the crabs' spawning behavior. Delaware Bay is a hotbed of horseshoe crab spawning, the greatest gathering of these creatures in the world.

When female horseshoe crabs arrive in the shallow waters of the bay, usually in late April or early May, they are met by sex-starved males. The male of the species is only about half the size of the female, and it possesses a special pair of pincers called pedipalpi, which it uses to grasp the female's carapace. Spawning usually takes place during a full-moon high tide.

As the tide starts to recede, the females begin to move toward the beach. A wall of males greets them, bumping around in the surf and scrambling on top of one another in their eagerness to find a mate. Their frantic struggles muddy the water, but males apparently don't use their nine eyes to identify females, but rather follow a chemical scent the females produce.

When a lucky male grabs a female as she hauls herself out on the beach, she pulls him through the sand like a locomotive pulls a boxcar. The female digs a nest six to eight inches deep in the sand below the high-tide line, where she deposits a cluster of four thousand or so eggs. Then she drags her still-attached mate over the nest so he can fertilize the eggs, which the pair then covers with sand.

However, the orgy is just beginning. Females carry eighty thousand or more eggs, and they continue to dig nests and bury eggs until spawning is done. Usually, this takes more than one day, and the females retreat to the shallow waters and come ashore again during a high tide. Sometimes, a waning tide strands a pair of joined crabs on the shore. At Kimbles Beach, I saw many such pairs burrowed into the sand waiting for the next tide to finish their business.

When the pair is finally done, thousands of BB-sized gray-green eggs lie buried beneath the sand. And this is what the shorebirds come to eat.

The abundance of wildlife at Delaware Bay during the three weeks or so of peak crab spawning is overwhelming. Hundred of thousands of horseshoe crabs lay hundreds of millions of eggs, which a million shorebirds come to eat. The numbers are staggering, but they are easier to swallow when reduced to a single bird.

A typical red knot arrives at the bay weighing slightly less than 4 ounces. When it leaves, it will weigh 6.3 ounces, a gain of over 60 percent. Many shorebirds will double their weight during their stay at Delaware Bay. The question is, How many crab eggs must a bird eat to gain that much weight?

The first part of the answer came in a 1989 paper by Castro, Myers, and Place. In a series of experiments, they fed seven captive sanderlings a steady diet of horseshoe crab eggs. One unpleasant part of the research was examining "in detail" the feces of the birds. Surprisingly, considering the birds' fondness for crab eggs, the researchers found that the eggs weren't assimilated well; over 70 percent passed through the birds' digestive tract unbroken. In fact, merely to maintain their body weight, each sanderling had to eat an astounding eighty-three hundred eggs per day. If the birds ate steadily for eight hours a day, they would have to consume an egg every four seconds. Clearly, migrating shorebirds needing to gain weight before continuing north would have to eat even more.

The second part of the answer came from Brian Harrington, who did the arithmetic for red knots. He concluded that each knot consumed 135,000 eggs during its two-week stopover at Delaware Bay, a rate of 4 eggs per second for birds on an eight-hour feeding schedule. My own calculations, based on Castro and Myers's 1993 paper, indicate that an even higher rate of consumption would be required. But no matter how you figure it, one bird clearly eats a lot of crab eggs. And every spring, a million shorebirds stop at Delaware Bay to feed on those eggs.

Altogether, Castro and Myers concluded, those shorebirds would consume over five hundred *tons* of crab eggs in a three-week period, if they ate nothing but crab eggs. However, the birds do supplement their diet with other foods—primarily arthropods and polychaete worms. Nevertheless, since each female lays only about ten ounces of eggs, a lot of crabs are necessary to furnish the food that fuels the shorebirds' northward migration. And some people believe that the number of spawning crabs in Delaware Bay is declining.

Because horseshoe crabs aren't edible or a threat to humans, you might think they would be safe from the kind of overfishing that devastated the cod on Georges Bank and the bluefin tuna in the deep waters off the eastern seaboard. Nothing could be further from the truth. The National Audubon Society reported that the number of crabs taken from Delaware Bay increased from 330,000 in 1993 to 800,000 in 1996.

Horseshoe crabs are gathered directly from the beaches during spawning, or they are netted by trawlers. They are sold as bait for conchs and eels, which are caught in traps. Large crabs are cut into quarters with a band saw before they are put into the traps. Eel fishermen prefer females because their eggs attract more fish. In 1998, the going price for horseshoe crabs was a dollar for a female, fifty cents for a male.

The increased take of crabs has birders up in arms. They fear that a declining population of crabs will harm Delaware Bay's shorebirds. But another group is equally concerned; the biomedical industry also has an interest in maintaining horseshoe crab numbers. It turns out that the crabs' unique copper-based, infection-resistant blood has a constituent that is useful in medicine. But this exciting discovery was just the latest chapter in mankind's effort to find a use for horseshoe crabs.

L. polyphemus was first described by Thomas Harriot in the 1590 edition of *A Briefe and True Report of the New Found Land of Virginia*. There, among the "Trouts, Porpoises, Rayes . . . and many other sortes of excellent good fish" is the "Seekanauk," or horsefoot crab. It was, he wrote, "a kind of crustie shell fishe which is good meate, about a foote in breadth, having a crustie tayle, many legs like a crab; and her eyes in her backe." The "good meate" was an overstatement, perhaps designed to entice settlers to the New World. In fact, about the only use American Indians made of the horseshoe crab was to tip their arrows with the sharp end of its tail.

But European settlers weren't about to let such a plentiful resource go unused, even if it was inedible. By the mid-nineteenth century, a thriving industry developed in which horseshoe crabs were ground up for poultry feed and fertilizer. In one year in the 1870s, over 4,000,000 crabs were taken from the beaches of New Jersey and Delaware and sent to grinding factories. Delaware's Slaughter Beach got its name from the grim business of collecting horseshoe crabs for those factories. Predictably, the number of crabs declined. Shuster and Botton reported that the annual harvest in the 1950s averaged only 115,000 crabs.

As the fertilizer industry petered out, along came a biomedical break-through that would prove far less lethal to crabs and far more important to humans than arrow tips and fertilizer. Dr. Frederick Bang was working at Woods Hole Biological Laboratory in Massachusetts when he discovered accidentally that the blood of horseshoe crabs clotted when exposed to bacterial endotoxins.

Those endotoxins (and the bacteria associated with them) can be found almost anywhere—in our drinking water and our intestines, for example, where they do no harm. But if endotoxins enter the bloodstream, the results are often fatal. Diseases such as spinal meningitis and toxic shock syndrome are caused by endotoxins.

At the time, the best way to test for endotoxin-related infections was to inject samples of suspected blood (or urine or spinal fluid) into a rabbit. If the rabbit developed a fever or died, the patient was treated with antibodies to control the disease. Unfortunately, it could take up to forty-eight hours to get results, a sometimes dangerous delay. As Dr. Bang knew, a quicker test would save lives.

Bang was joined by Jack Levin. Together, they made a reagent from horseshoe crab blood called *Limulus* amoebocyte lysate, or LAL. The idea was to provide hospitals and doctors a simple test to detect endotoxin contamination of surgical equipment, hypodermic needles, and vaccines—all common sources of human infection.

In 1976, LAL detected the presence of endotoxins in swine flu vaccine. The subsequent widespread use of LAL, Thomas Novitsky wrote, has "resulted in a dramatic improvement in the quality of drugs and biological products for intravenous injection." Dr. Bang, a modest man, attributed his discovery to serendipity, but medical historians credit him for investigating a minor incident that many scientists might have ignored: the unexpected clotting of a horseshoe crab's blood.

Today, several companies bleed crabs to make commercial quantities of LAL. After bleeding, a procedure that kills about 10 percent of the crabs, the survivors are released back into the water. The companies depend on a readily available supply of horseshoe crabs, so they—along with birders and fishermen—have a stake in the Delaware Bay crab population. And when that population began to decline, each group was out to protect its own interests.

Urged on by birders and the manufacturers of LAL (but opposed by many fishermen), New Jersey and Delaware restricted horseshoe crab harvests. Then the Atlantic States Marine Fisheries Commission agreed to develop a plan to manage and conserve the horseshoe crab along the East Coast. The job of sorting out the often-conflicting data to determine if crab populations really were declining—and if so, by how much—was assigned to a team of state and federal biologists, which was to propose a horseshoe crab management plan to the commission. And because he was available and qualified, the job of writing the management plan was assigned to Eric Schrading, a biologist at the United States Fish and Wildlife Service's Pleasantville, New Jersey, office.

Eric is a tall young man with closely cropped hair and informal, preppie clothes. The Ivy League look is misleading, though; Eric is from Pittsburgh, and he got his master's degree in wildlife biology at Virginia Polytechnic Institute, where his thesis involved tracking raccoons in southwestern Virginia.

We meet in a cluttered conference room near his office. Beside his coffee cup is a neat stack of papers. We begin going through them. Eric produces graph after graph, table after table; he talks about horseshoe crab egg data, horseshoe crab spawning data, horseshoe crab trawl data. The living creatures I saw yesterday at Kimbles Beach have been reduced to wildly fluctuating numbers and erratic lines on graphs. The data has flaws: methods of counting have changed from year to year; some years are missing; trawling gear has changed. When I point this out, Eric nods in agreement.

"You're right," he says. "The data isn't good. But most data sets show that crab populations in Delaware Bay have declined in the last several years. If you wait to make a management decision based on a perfect data set, then you might be looking at the next passenger pigeon."

"Do you have any shorebird data?" I ask.

Eric pulls out a bar graph, the unpublished results of aerial surveys conducted by employees of the New Jersey Endangered and Nongame Species Program. The raw data is volatile, but the trend is clearly downward. At the bottom of the page is a conclusion: "While the number of shorebirds varies annually, there has been a statistically significant decline in the number of birds since 1986."

"Do you believe this?"

Eric shuffles his papers and pulls out yet another graph. "Yes," he replies. "Other data confirm the decline."

"And the declining crab population caused this?"

"Maybe. No one knows for sure. But if it wasn't for the shorebirds, the plight of the crabs would be a very low-priority issue. Birds are more charismatic," he says with a wry grin.

"Yesterday, Kimbles Beach was packed with birds."

"Right," he says, and for the first time, I hear a hint of frustration in his voice. "Everybody has their own anecdotal evidence. One person says, 'I'm a member of the Audubon Society, and I remember walking on the beach in 1990 and seeing thousands of crabs. Now there's none.' And on the other side, you've got the commercial fisherman that says, 'I've been fishing here in this bay for twenty-five years, and I've never seen so many horseshoe crabs as this year.' Everybody has a different view. Sure, I'm glad they're interested, and I'm glad they're noticing the crabs, but you can't use that kind of evidence in your population assessment. You just can't rely on it."

As we continue to plow through the data, it becomes clear that both crabs and birds in Delaware Bay have declined in the last few years. But the numbers are too scattered for Eric to say by how much.

"Overharvesting isn't the crabs' only problem," he says. "Shoreline erosion and development, including the bulkheads and groins that come with it, continue to reduce horseshoe crab spawning habitat. But it could be worse. Some fisheries make decisions with a lot less data than we have. Ultimately, it comes to a philosophy. If you really don't know, do you take the conservative line and say, 'We're going to pull back crab harvests until we have a better feel for what's going on'? Or do you say, 'We don't have enough data to make a decision, therefore we're going to continue to harvest as is'?"

"So," I ask, "what will happen after you turn the management plan over to the commission?"

"New Jersey and Delaware have already restricted crab harvests. The commission could make all states comply with an even more restrictive plan. They could set quotas."

"Do you think that will happen?"

Eric leans back in his chair and looks up, as if the answer might be written on the ceiling. "I have no idea," he says finally.

Bruce Luebke, Fish and Wildlife's man at Cape May National Wildlife Refuge, parks his truck at Kimbles Beach. Cape May is part of the Edwin B. Forsythe complex of refuges, and though Bruce's title is assistant manager, he is the only person who actually spends his days at the Cape May refuge.

The blue sky over Delaware Bay is filled with shorebirds flying in tight formation, their colors changing from dark to light to flashing silver as they wheel and bank in the morning sun. This beach is only a small part of the refuge. Bruce has already shown me the inland sections, which are mostly cedar swamps and second-growth forests that lie well away from the bay. But this short beach segment and a few others like it are clearly the refuge's primary reason for being.

Cape May is famous for birds, especially the raptors that fly south down the peninsula in the fall and often hesitate before crossing the open waters of Delaware Bay, giving hawk watchers good views. The area is routinely listed as one of the top ten birding sites in America and proudly proclaims itself the "Raptor Capital of the United States." It is also famous for its birders. Pete Dunne, Clay Sutton, and others were chronicled in Jack Connor's *Season at the Point*; they are as well known here as movie stars are in Hollywood.

Because of the profusion of birds and birders, the Cape May peninsula has many natural areas and wildlife sanctuaries. The Nature Conservancy has at least a half-dozen preserves; the state has six wildlife management areas and three state parks, including the world-famous Cape May Point State Park; and Cape May County maintains several small natural areas and a zoo. To further support wildlife and wildlife viewers, the New Jersey Audubon Society runs three visitor centers on the peninsula. Missing from this list until recently was the United States Fish and Wildlife Service, which didn't get around to establishing a refuge here until 1989, making Bruce Luebke the new kid on the block.

Bruce is a solidly built Minnesotan with a prematurely receding hairline and a degree in wildlife management from the University of Wisconsin at Stevens Point. He speaks slowly and chooses his words carefully. If he isn't sure how to respond to a question, he says so, and when he does answer one, you get the feeling you can take it to the bank. And despite being a newcomer to the area, he understands what has to be done at the refuge.

"There's not much we can do here on the beach except educate the public and try to minimize the disturbance to the birds. The refuge doesn't own the beach; all property up to the mean high-tide line belongs to the state. It's public land, open to fishing and hiking. Several sites on the beaches are already designated as viewing areas, and we encourage birders to go to those places.

"Shorebirds depend on crab eggs, and the refuge has no control over crab harvests. Maybe we can influence the management plan that Eric is putting together. Until then, we have one main objective at this refuge. Come on, I'll show you."

We ride to Bruce's office, a mile or so away. On the wall is a large map with refuge properties marked. The properties are scattered haphazardly across the map. "This is the problem," Bruce says. "We need to connect the protected lands, to make the refuge whole. Our goal is to double the size of the refuge. We want more beachfront, but other types of habitat are important, too."

The map has two long ovals drawn on either side of Highway 47, the state road that runs north and south on the western side of the Cape May peninsula. To the west of the highway are marshes and beaches; to the east are forests. When the acquisition program is completed, these properties will give shorebirds, raptors, and songbirds a mosaic of protected habitats.

Although the main attraction for shorebirds in spring is crab eggs, some scientists believe that these other habitats are also essential to them. That hypothesis was presented in 1996 by Burger, Niles, and Clark. After studying the shorebirds of Cape May, they concluded that the birds feed nearly constantly. Thus, at high tide, when water covers the sand where the crab eggs are buried, the birds move from the beaches to the mud flats and marshes. And if Cape May National Wildlife Refuge expands as planned, those habitats will be protected.

I remember my first day at Kimbles Beach. The tide was high, and the shore was packed with resting shorebirds. Clearly, if enough horseshoe crab eggs are available, the birds prefer them to hunting and pecking through marshes and mud flats, just as most of us would prefer a breakfast buffet to sifting through the straw in a chicken coop for our eggs. Furthermore, the birds appeared to be willing to wait on the beach for the tide to recede.

This speculation was confirmed in an unpublished paper by Tsipoura and Burger, which concluded that the diet of shorebirds at Cape May "consists mainly of horseshoe crab eggs." As one would suspect, it's no accident that the shorebirds arrive at Delaware Bay at the peak of the horseshoe crab spawning season.

What would happen to one million shorebirds if the population of crabs at Delaware Bay were to drop precipitously? The biggest problem they'd encounter would be finding the eggs that had been laid. Remember, crabs deposit their eggs six to eight inches below the surface of the sand, too deep for the short beaks of common shorebirds to reach them. (Of all the shorebirds at Delaware Bay, only ruddy turnstones dig in the sand for eggs, and that technique works only if the beach is densely packed with eggs.)

Shorebirds rely on the crabs themselves (and an occasional storm) to make the eggs accessible. As wave after wave of spawning crabs dig nests in the sandy beaches, they uncover eggs laid by earlier spawners. These eggs lie on or near the surface, and they are the ones shorebirds eat. Because these eggs are exposed, they would never hatch anyway, which is why feeding shorebirds have little impact on crab populations. To expose these superfluous eggs requires what Eric Schrading calls a "critical density" of crabs. No one knows what that density is, but if the crab population isn't high enough, far fewer eggs will be available to hungry shorebirds.

That may have been the situation in the 1920s and 1930s, when the enormous harvests of previous decades apparently depleted the crabs' numbers. I use the word *apparently* because no census data is available from those years. All we really know is that crab harvests from Delaware Bay generally declined from the 1870s to the 1970s, according to Shuster and Botton; in the 1960s, harvests were only a fraction of those in the 1870s. In one of the few early censuses, Shuster and Botton estimated a population of 273,000 spawning crabs on the shores of Delaware Bay in 1977, which they said was "several fold larger than that which existed during the 1960s."

Shorebird data is equally scant. Probably the best source is Witmer Stone's remarkable book, *Bird Studies at Old Cape May*. Stone was born in Philadelphia in 1866. After graduating from the University of Pennsylvania, he began a fruitful fifty-year association with the Academy of Natural Sciences of Philadelphia, where he held many positions, including curator of North American birds. He was by all accounts a kindly man with wide-ranging interests in the natural world. He was also a respected scientist who became editor of *The Auk*, the journal of the American Ornithologists' Union.

In 1890, Stone and four other men organized the Delaware Valley Ornithological Club. His book contains his own detailed observations of forty-eight years in and around Cape May, as well as the observations of members of the club and others. These birders carefully documented their sightings—species, locations, dates, numbers, weather—and Witmer Stone dutifully recorded them. But nowhere in the 941 pages of the two-volume edition did he mention a great spring congregation of shorebirds feeding on horseshoe crab eggs.

Could the members of the Delaware Valley Ornithological Club have missed 1,000,000 or so shorebirds? It's possible but unlikely. Stone and his associates were thoroughly familiar with all of the common shorebirds and recorded their comings and goings. The dates logged for the birds' spring arrival at Cape May were the same as the dates they arrive today. But the numbers of birds spotted in their peak counts were far lower than today's censuses: 500 red knots on May 26, 1929; 12 on May 23, 1930; 150 on May 24, 1931. The members of other species—ruddy turnstones, semipalmated sandpipers, and sanderlings—occasionally reached a count of 4,000, but they never came close to Pete Dunne's one-day count of nearly 500,000 shorebirds.

Similarly, Stone never mentioned the great gathering of horseshoe crabs that we see today. Nor did he mention shorebirds feeding on their eggs, although he quoted one man who observed that ruddy turnstones flew "back and forth across Cape May to feed on king [horseshoe] crabs which are washed up in numbers on the bay shore."

In any case, it seems unlikely that shorebirds stopping at Cape May were as abundant in the early part of this century as they are today. One reason was market and sport hunting of shorebirds, which wasn't stopped until 1916. The birds' recovery was likely restrained by the number of spawning crabs, which was much lower than it is today, due to overharvesting for fertilizer.

To put it simply, fewer crabs mean fewer eggs, and fewer eggs mean fewer birds. Furthermore, there is little Bruce Luebke or the Fish and Wildlife Service can do about it. In fact, Bruce is facing a problem that is common to managers of most sanctuaries: he doesn't fully control his own destiny. No matter how well he does his job, no matter how much land he acquires, he can't ensure that enough crabs will make it to the beaches to supply the birds with sufficient eggs for their migration.

Though many species are endangered because of loss of habitat, sometimes species, not habitats, need direct protection, which is why we have the much-maligned Endangered Species Act. Of course, even at their current reduced population, horseshoe crabs aren't endangered. And the regulations needed to protect them can't be enacted by Fish and Wildlife or Bruce Luebke. The crabs must rely on decisions reached by the Atlantic States Marine Fisheries Commission.

The next morning, I return to Kimbles Beach. It's low tide, and the beach is littered with horseshoe crabs, most of them alive and upside down. Supposedly, the crabs use their telsons to right themselves when they become upended. That technique may work in the water, but on the beach, they appear helpless. Without thinking, I grab the nearest crab and tip it over. It begins a slow crawl down the beach to the sea, bulldozing its way through the sand.

These are primitive creatures. Because they have relatively simple eyes and a four-inch-long optic nerve, Dr. H. Keffer Hartline selected horseshoe crabs to study the mechanics of vision. He discovered that electrical impulses flowed through the optic nerve from eye to brain. Much of what we know about vision today started with this work, which won Hartline a Nobel Prize in 1967.

But later work showed that the vision of a horseshoe crab isn't as simple as Dr. Hartline supposed. A horseshoe crab can see at night because of a complicated interaction between its simple eyes, its compound eyes, and its biological clock—the same clock that tells it when to move into the shallow waters of Delaware Bay to spawn. This clock is more accurate than any timepiece in the human brain.

In fact, the horseshoe crab may be primitive, but it is not simple. Crab blood is very complex, which is why the biomedical industry relies on extracts from it, rather than on synthesizing the chemicals that make the blood sensitive to endotoxins. The horseshoe crab also has unique gills that resemble the pages of a book, and though it usually gets from place to place by crawling on the seabed, when it does swim, it flips over and does a backstroke. And unlike its closest relatives, the spiders, *L. polyphemus* is slow to reach sexual maturity. Females don't spawn until they are nine years old, and they have a life expectancy of fourteen to eighteen years.

Shuster and Botton have pointed out that populations of slow-maturing, long-lived species tend to be more stable than those of shorter-lived species. But they also said that if such a species is "heavily harvested, it may take longer to repopulate an area." This could account for the low crab population in Delaware Bay in the 1950s and 1960s, when the crabs were still recovering from the exorbitant harvests of the fertilizer industry.

Clearly, if we want to sustain all of the people and birds that depend on horseshoe crabs, we will have to reduce harvests. Although crabs are still numerous, overharvesting or loss of habitat will eventually deplete their population. This happened in Japan, when diking and filling of beaches destroyed most of the spawning habitat of *Tachypleus tridentatus*, the once-abundant horseshoe crab found there. Today, the species is so rare that the Japanese consider it a national treasure.

For shorebirds and the biomedical industry, for conch and eel fishermen, and indeed for itself, *L. polyphemus* deserves a similar status in the United States. Let's hope that we don't have to repeat the Japanese experience to recognize the horseshoe crab's value.

Note: Just before this book went to press, the Atlantic States Marine Fisheries Commission rejected the coast-wide restrictions on horseshoe crab harvests proposed by Eric Schrading and the other members of the Horseshoe Crab Plan Development Team. It said that more data is needed.

CHAPTER 5

The Surviving Auk
Machias Seal Island, New Brunswick, Canada

JONESPORT, MAINE, 7 A.M. Captain Barna B. Norton eases the big inboard away from the dock. It is early July. It is foggy. It is cold. The horizon is a theoretical line where gray fog merges with gray water. "Best weather we've had in a month," says Barna cheerfully, gunning the boat into the teeth of the wind. Diane, my heat-loving wife, settles miserably in a partially protected corner of the open cockpit. I sit stoically with the other passengers in the rear of the boat.

As we ride, the fog begins to lift. Stubby birds with stubby wings race beside the boat. Terns flutter and hover, then dive into the sea. After an hour of running flat-out on calm seas, Barna eases back on the throttle. A rocky shore rises from the water. A short, white lighthouse appears in the center of a tiny island. Beneath it are three low-slung, red-roofed buildings. Birds of all shapes and sizes paddle through the sea around us, and clouds of terns swirl above the island. This great concentration of bird life is one reason I wanted to come to Machias Seal Island.

There are other reasons, too. At only fifteen acres, Machias Seal Island lies at one extreme of a hot debate that has occupied many ecologists during the last three decades. The argument was (and is) over the optimum size of nature preserves. One group of ecologists believes that a few big preserves are preferable to a lot of small ones. Another group disagrees. It has become known as the SLOSS debate, an acronym for Single Large Or Several Small. I hope that an on-site interview with the manager of Machias Seal Island might shed some light on the problems of a small wildlife preserve—and how he or she deals with them.

Machias also appeals to me because it is a southern stronghold of a family of diving birds known as the alcids. Even today, over 150 years after it disappeared from earth, the most famous member of that family is the great auk. I became interested in auks back in the 1960s after I read a novel, *The Great Auk*, an anthropomorphic (but reasonably accurate) tearjerker that made a lasting impression on an impressionable young man. And one of the great auk's closest relatives—the surviving auk—nests on Machias Seal Island.

The great auk was a flightless black-and-white bird that stood about two feet tall. It was a powerful swimmer, but its ungainly, wobbling gait made it helpless on land. It was also fat and tasty, which made it a target for human consumption. When great auks came ashore to nest in the summer, they were systematically slaughtered by North Atlantic fishermen for their feathers and meat. There was no need to waste gunpowder on the awkward auks; sailors simply walked ashore and clubbed them to death.

As the great auk became rare, the museums of the world decided that they needed specimens for their collections. The last known auk breeding site was Eldey Island, just off the southwestern coast of Iceland. In 1830, twenty or twenty-one birds were "collected." In 1831, the tally was twenty-four. Nine more were killed in 1834. By 1840, collectors managed only one egg, but the following year, they got three birds and one egg. The last two great auks ever seen alive were killed on Eldey Island by Jon Brandsson and Sigourour Isleffson on June 3, 1844. For reasons that remain incomprehensible, Ketil Kittelsson smashed the egg that the pair had produced. The great auk was extinct.

The twenty-three surviving species of the family Alcidae all inhabit the inhospitable northern seas, from the North Atlantic and the Arctic Ocean to the Bering Sea and the North Pacific. They are often called the "penguins of the north" because they resemble those birds of the austral seas, but to be historically accurate, the reverse is actually the case. The original penguin was the great auk.

The great auk's scientific name is *Pinguinus impennis*. The genus name came from the great auk's common name, *penguin*, which was given to it by early explorers and was probably derived from the Welch words *pen* and *gwyn*, meaning white-headed. When later explorers encountered a southern, cold-loving, flightless diving bird that also had a white patch on its head, it reminded them of the great auk, and they named it—what else?—*penguin*.

Actually, auks and penguins—which closely resemble one another in appearance and behavior—are not closely related. They developed their similarities through the process of convergent evolution, in which two entirely different lineages produce similar organisms to fill similar ecological niches. Chimney swifts and brown bats both have wings, roost in dark places, and pick off flying insects, but their evolutionary histories are obviously quite different.

In any case, although the southern penguin closely resembles the great auk, the bird that is actually more closely related to it is the razorbill, which can be found on Machias Seal Island.

Barna's son John, a tall, bearded man who spelled his father at the helm on the way over, runs us ashore in a dinghy moored near the island. Barna, still nimble at age eighty-three, leads us up a slippery, algae-covered concrete ramp. He holds an umbrella over his head with an American flag sticking out of the top. Both flag and umbrella have a purpose.

Barna disputes the claim that Machias is a Canadian island. He believes it belongs to the United States, and the flag is a not-so-subtle reminder to the Canadian Wildlife Service, which manages the island, that he does not accept its sovereignty. The umbrella is protection from the swarms of Arctic terns that nest on the island.

Arctic terns are beautiful birds, mostly white with black-capped heads and blood-red, stiletto-like beaks. They soar above us on slender wings, screeching loudly and preparing to dive-bomb any human intruders who encroach on their nesting grounds.

Barna hands each passenger a thin wooden stick, which we dutifully hold over our heads as instructed. The theory is that the terns will attack the stick rather that your head. On this day, the theory holds, because we all scamper along a boardwalk through the nesting area without anyone's scalp getting creased by an irate tern.

Each tern nest is marked by a small flag. Some of them are less than ten feet from the boardwalks that crisscross the island. Beneath the flags are baby terns. The chicks are only a few days old, and adult terns come and go regularly, stuffing food down the throats of those pleading balls of brown fluff.

After watching the terns for a few minutes, we are led to little gray boxes that look like outhouses but serve as blinds. Diane and I settle inside one and close the door. After a minute or two, she slides open one of the peepholes.

The fog has lifted, and the blue sky is filled with terns. Beneath them is a jumble of gray boulders. Groups of odd-looking birds stand erect on virtually every surface. A cacophony of screeches and whistles and low growls fills the salty, fishy-smelling air.

The birds are so close that I don't need my binoculars to identify them: puffins and razorbills. Both species are more accomplished on land than the great auk, but they are far from graceful. They waddle from rock to rock. With their black-and-white plumage, they look like a bunch of drunks wearing tuxedos.

Atlantic puffins (*Fratercula arctica*) are the glamour species on Machias. Almost everyone who visits comes to see puffins. And they are—there's no other word for it—*cute*. Puffins are chunky birds with stubby wings, bright orange feet and legs, and an oversized orange beak that in profile forms a nearly perfect equilateral triangle. Even serious ornithologists can't resist calling them "sea parrots."

One reason for their popularity is their lack of skittishness. Puffins wander to within a foot or two of our blind, allowing Diane to take enough puffin pictures to last a lifetime. Some of them have a half-dozen or so silvery fish held crosswise in their big, colorful beaks. They disappear beneath the rocks into the burrows where they nest, presumably to feed their chicks.

When something spooks the puffins, they take off with a noticeable *whir*, short wings beating madly and curious orange feet trailing behind, seemingly an afterthought. Every so often, one lands on the roof of our blind, and we can hear it walking above us, feet flapping.

A few razorbills mingle with the puffins, but they often stand alone, as if waiting for something or someone. Compared to the comical puffins, razorbills are models of decorum.

The razorbill (*Alca torda*) is a duck-sized bird, larger than a puffin but smaller than a great auk. Its coloration—black on top with a white breast—is identical to that of its extinct relative, except that it lacks the white patch above the eye. Its plumage is so tight that it appears to be painted on its body, rather than being composed of individual feathers. Its black eyes, set in an all-black head, are difficult to make out even with the aid of binoculars. The razorbill's thick, black beak carries the same curious white striping that the great auk's did.

Razorbills are colonial nesters, laying one egg, usually on bare rock in whatever enclosed space they can find. On Machias, they generally nest in crevices beneath the boulders. So well concealed are their nests that we never spotted a single razorbill egg or chick during our stay.

Like all of the alcids, razorbills are diving birds. Their black, webbed feet are set far back on their bodies. That positioning gives them their erect posture and awkward gait on land, but it also allows their feet to act as rudders during a dive. Their short wings require them to flap mightily to stay aloft, but they are amazingly efficient in the water. They can dive to great depths in pursuit of the small fish that they prefer. In one experiment, published in the *Journal of Zoology, London*, one razorbill dove well over three hundred feet—and that was with a radio transmitter attached to its back.

According to statistics compiled by The Nature Conservancy, more species are in danger of extinction because of habitat loss than for any other reason. But that's today. Over the past four or five hundred years, most North American extinctions were caused by slaughter, pure and simple. The passenger pigeon, for example, was wiped out by humans with guns and clubs. So were the great auk and other species. The razorbill almost experienced the same fate. And as was the case with the great auk, the principal cause of its decline was the once-ubiquitous codfish.

The Grand Banks lie just east of Newfoundland. At one time, those cold, shallow waters were home to the richest cod fishery in the world. One of the first Europeans to encounter the Grand Banks was an Italian named Giovanni Caboto, who was renamed John Cabot by the English. In 1497, only five years after Columbus's maiden voyage, Cabot reported that "the sea is covered with fishes." Soon, huge fleets were sailing from Europe to the New World in search of codfish, whose firm, white flesh could be salted, frozen, or dried.

In those days, cod fishing was done with hand lines, and the favored bait was seabirds. Acquiring the bait was simple. John James Audubon, who visited the Canadian coast in 1833, recorded the fishermen's technique:

> The fishermen who kill these birds to get their flesh for codfish
> bait, ascend in parties of six or eight, armed with clubs. . . . As they

reach the top, the birds, alarmed, rise with a noise like thunder, and fly off in such hurried, fearful confusion as to throw each other down, often falling on each other till there is a bank of them many feet high. The men strike them down and kill them until fatigued or satisfied. Five hundred and forty have been thus murdered in one hour by six men. The birds are skinned with little care, and the flesh cut off in chunks. . . . So great is the destruction of these birds annually that their flesh supplies the bait for upwards of forty fishing boats.

Bait wasn't the only use cod fishermen had for northern seabirds. They were also a reliable source of fresh meat and eggs. Their feathers were stuffed into pillows and mattresses, and great auks' flesh furnished oil for lamps. Audubon himself tried razorbill stew and pronounced it "good eating, much better than would be expected from birds of its class and species." But Audubon could see the writing on the wall. "In less than half a century," he wrote, "these wonderful nurseries will be entirely destroyed, unless some kind government will interfere to stop the shameless destruction."

Unfortunately, no kind government stepped forward. The result was one extinct alcid species and several devastated ones. One of the hardest hit was the razorbill. In 1912, ornithologist Arthur Cleveland Bent cruised the shores of Labrador searching for seabirds. He saw no razorbills in places where they had once been abundant and concluded that "the large breeding colonies of the Alcidae had been nearly, if not quite, annihilated on 'the Labrador.'"

Nonetheless, the razorbill did not follow its cousin, the great auk, to extinction. One reason was a difference in breeding habits. The great auk nested in dense colonies on only a few islands, and nothing could dissuade it from returning to those sites every summer. Those islands became convenience stores for cod fishermen, a place where they could stop, anchor their boats, and run ashore for fresh meat and eggs. The razorbill survived the worst of this slaughter because its nesting sites were more widely distributed. Furthermore, it was more agile on the ground, and it could fly—which made it harder to kill with clubs.

In 1916, the United States and Canada signed the Migratory Bird Treaty. It prohibited most takings of migratory birds (including alcids) and their eggs. Native Americans could still hunt alcids, and winter hunting of some species remained legal in parts of Canada. Nevertheless, the razorbill finally had some relief.

According to Nettleship and Evans, razorbill populations "remained low or continued to decrease up to the 1950s." This same trend was apparent at Machias, where razorbills "disappeared as nesters" until the early 1950s.

To find out how they stand today, I hunt down Jason Hudson, the Canadian Wildlife Service's warden on Machias Seal Island.

Jason is a slender young man with a neatly trimmed beard and thick glasses. He tells me that this is his fifth summer at Machias. Despite the coolness of the day, he is wearing shorts and sandals. A Canadian Wildlife Service patch adorns the chest of his windbreaker. We sit across from one another at a picnic table beneath the lighthouse, which begins *whoo*ing when an afternoon fog rolls in. Arctic terns swoop overhead, screeching loudly but not attacking. Jason, who is a bit of a diplomat, begins with one ground rule: "I'll tell you everything I know about the birds here, but I don't want to get into politics."

"You mean like who owns Machias?"

Jason frowns. "Yeah. Canada has had a lighthouse and lighthouse keepers here since about 1830. And we've had a summer warden here since 1971. That's good enough for me."

"Me, too. Besides, I'm more interested in birds. And Canada seems to be doing a good job with them. Lots of terns, puffins, and razorbills. Do you have census data?"

Jason, who has not a scrap of paper with him, reels off the following numbers from counts done the previous month: 2,975 pairs of terns, 70 percent Arctic, 30 percent common; 1,500 pairs of puffins; between 300 and 500 pairs of razorbills.

I do the arithmetic in my head: nearly 10,000 birds on this fifteen-acre rock. To give myself time to think about the incredibly high density of birds, I ask another question: "Any other species here?"

"We also have Leach's storm petrels, between 50 and 100 pairs. But that's an uncertain number. Their burrows are impossible to census. And visitors never see any because they're nocturnal. They're either at sea or in their burrows during the day. You only really see them at night. We also have about 132 common eiders."

Finally, I blurt out what's bothering me. "Ten thousand birds. On this island? That's amazing."

"It's not the island," Jason says. "The birds only nest here. The eco-system that supports them is out there." He waves his hand in a circle.

"The sea," I say. "Of course. But I heard in Jonesport that the herring fishery was down back in the seventies, and that the terns starved." Actually, I heard that the Canadian government had financed purse seiners in the North Atlantic, and that they had fished out the herring. But like Jason, I am trying to avoid politics.

Jason starts slowly. "I don't know all the ins and outs, but we probably depleted the stocks a lot. But we can't deplete them to the point that there's none left. Although we did with the cod, so that's probably a wrong statement."

Jason is referring to the Grand Banks, where the cod were fished out, devastating the economy of fishing villages that had relied on them for centuries. A similar collapse occurred in the United States on Georges Bank. So far, though, the North Atlantic herring fishery has escaped that disaster. "Well, the herring must have rebounded. There's plenty of terns."

"Yeah," Jason says. "Hake and herring are the two main fish the birds bring in."

"Machias appears to be doing well. Could anything go wrong?"

Jason hesitates. As with most on-the-ground wildlife managers, he has seen so many predictions go awry that he is reluctant to speculate. Ask an on-site wildlife biologist if the sun will rise in the east, and he or she will say, "Well, it did yesterday, so it might tomorrow."

"There are so many things you can think of," Jason says. "What if someone in Africa decides to start eating terns?"

Finally, he loosens up a bit. "Cold, wet weather can kill newly hatched tern chicks. Herring and hake could be overfished or suffer natural disaster. And what happens during the winter when the birds are at sea?"

"What about visitors?" I ask.

He explains the system by which two of the island's three vendors are allowed to transport visitors to Machias on any given day. "It's a thirty-person-per-day limit. Only three charter boats are allowed to visit. They can bring a total of up to twenty-six passengers. Four more can come ashore from private boats. Visitors don't appear to be doing any damage, but we wouldn't want to see more."

"Do gulls do any damage? They eat tern eggs and chicks, I'm told."

"That's a problem. But the terns usually keep them off."

"You're not doing anything?" I ask the question because I know that some lighthouse keepers shot gulls in the old days.

For the first time today, Jason smiles. "How do I answer that? I do scare gulls on occasion. But a bigger worry is oil spills. We have tankers going by . . ."

"What are your goals here? What are you working on? Trying to improve?"

The day's visitors are heading our way, walking rapidly down the boardwalk from the blinds, holding their sticks in the air to decoy the ever-alert, ever-aggressive terns. Jason gets up from the picnic table. "We'd like to leave it the way it is. You can always improve things, but right now, we're in good shape. I want to keep it that way."

The widespread decline of razorbills that took place during the last century has been halted. Today, about seven hundred thousand razorbills are scattered across the North Atlantic from Scotland to Canada, and the population is believed to be stable. Nevertheless, the species is subject to disaster. Thousands die from oil spills and starvation. So frequent are these occurrences that ornithologists have given them a name: *wrecks.*

One such wreck occurred off the east coast of England and Scotland in February 1983. Over thirty thousand seabirds, about two-thirds of them razorbills (the others were mostly guillemots, another alcid), washed ashore. Only 5 percent were oiled; the rest died of starvation, apparently when bad weather pushed them into waters where fish were small and scarce.

But compared to deaths caused by humans, natural disasters are a mere drop in the ocean. Evans and Nettleship listed the threats to alcids in *The Atlantic Alcidae*: hunting (both legal and illegal) still takes a toll, especially in Greenland; thousands die each year when they become entangled in fishing nets; floating factories that process fish deplete the schools that alcids eat; and herring and black-backed gulls, whose populations have exploded in some areas because they feed on the offal from fishing boats, prey on alcid eggs and chicks.

One of the problems that alcids don't face is the threat that The Nature Conservancy considers most worrisome: habitat loss. There's still plenty of ocean, and the lands on which alcids breed and nest are unsuitable for agriculture or development. But though there's plenty of habitat available, we humans sometimes foul it.

The biggest threat to many alcids—including the razorbill—is oil pollution. Major oil spills—like the *Exxon Valdez*, for example—grab headlines around the world, but smaller spills often go unnoticed. Over a seventeen-year period from January 1966 to February 1983, fifty-three spills occurred in the North Atlantic that caused five hundred or more bird deaths each. The largest of these was the *Amoco Cadiz*, which dumped nearly a quarter of a million barrels of oil into the North Sea. But smaller spills also kill birds. Over thirty-five thousand birds died in an oil spill off the coast of Denmark, and no one even knows the name of the ship that caused it. The solution, Evans and Nettleship concluded, is government action to prevent and quickly clean up such spills.

In fact, timely government action in the form of laws and sanctuaries is the biggest weapon in the conservationists' arsenal. The birds of Machias Seal Island, for example, owe their abundance, and perhaps their existence, to the Canadian government.

As we are getting ready to leave Machias, one of that government's employees, a young man with a scraggly blond beard, comes out of the lighthouse, sits on a handy rock, and begins to play the violin. I don't recognize the tune, but it is a mournful one, a lament about something or someone. He is, Jason tells me, the current keeper of the Machias Seal Island lighthouse.

Canada assigned the first lighthouse keeper to Machias in 1832. Soon afterward, the harbor seals for which the island was named retreated to North Rock, a deserted shoal where they remain to this day. In those early years, the keeper was expected to support himself and whatever family he had with him. He brought cows for milk, sheep for meat, and dogs and cats for companionship. Some of the lighthouse keepers enjoyed the island's bird life and drove off the predatory gulls to protect the puffins and terns and razorbills. Others were not so accommodating. One keeper so disliked all the resident species that his successor reported he "shot every bird he saw."

After Canada designated Machias Seal Island as a migratory bird refuge in 1944, the birds no longer had to depend upon the kindness of lighthouse keepers. They were protected by the Canadian Wildlife Service. Since then, most of the island's bird populations have grown, including razorbills and puffins.

But everybody doesn't agree that government protection has helped. Chief among them is Captain Barna B. Norton, the skipper who ferried us to Machias.

I meet with Barna (pronounced "Bahna") at his house in Jonesport. It is a gray-shingled Cape Cod trimmed in white and surrounded by a lush, green lawn. The house is on the water. From the kitchen, you can see the town harbor and, beyond that, the Gulf of Maine. Barna was born in Jonesport in 1915, and he has lived here all his life except for a stint in the Coast Guard during World War II. He makes his living taking visitors to Machias Seal Island to see puffins, and his house is filled with images of his favorite bird: puffin photographs, puffin statues, puffins crocheted on pillows, and a drawing of a puffin with a red line through it and a caption that reads, "No Puffin'."

Barna is an impish man with thinning gray hair and a keen sense of humor. He is at war with the Canadian Wildlife Service over the ownership of Machias Seal Island, which he believes belongs to the United States.

"Before the Canadian Wildlife Service took over, the island was in good shape," he says before I can ask a question. "The lighthouse keepers shot the gulls and took care of the place. It's illegal to shoot gulls now."

"But more puffins live on the island now than before C.W.S. took over."

"My parents came here from Martha's Vineyard in 1860," Barna says. "They reported seeing lots of sea parrots. Still, I helped C.W.S. when they first came to Machias in 1971. Their head man came on a day when a hundred people were on the island. I brought forty, and Peter Wilcox"— one of the other vendors who ferries passengers to Machias—"had sixty. The C.W.S. man looked around and said, 'There's too many people here. They're disturbing the birds.' He asked me how many should be allowed ashore, and I told him twenty-five a day. And that's how the system we have today got started."

"That decision restricted you to thirteen passengers per trip. Didn't that cost you money?"

"Yes. But I didn't mind. I wanted to see the island protected. After all, it belongs to the United States. Look at this map."

Barna produces a map and several file folders of documents, all of which he believes prove his case. "Did you know that Machias has the only manned lighthouse in Canada?" he asks with a wicked smile. "Why would that be?"

I get the feeling that this is a standard joke, so I play the straight man. "I have no idea."

"They think I'll take it over if they leave."

Actually, Barna and the Canadian Wildlife Service have a good working relationship. He takes the warden and the lighthouse keeper their mail and speaks highly of Jason Hudson. But he isn't kidding about who owns the place. And though he's a little old for an invasion, he is still an energetic man, so Canada's probably right in keeping someone on the island.

Machias Seal Island harbors no endangered species. However, it is home to several that have been extirpated from, or dramatically reduced in, the Gulf of Maine. Over ten thousand birds breed on that fifteen-acre rock, whose market value is probably less than a year's rent on a modest New York apartment. And like New York real estate, what makes Machias valuable is location, location, location. An identical island a few hundred miles to the south would have no puffins or razorbills.

Small sanctuaries such as Machias play a significant role in the preservation of North America's wildlife. As we have seen, every monarch butterfly in eastern North America winters in areas that total only a few hundred acres in size. In places like Machias, one can easily grasp the practical issues raised by the SLOSS debate. A visit there suggests an inescapable conclusion: Under the right conditions, small preserves can be quite effective in protecting wildlife.

As Jason Hudson pointed out, one key to operating a small sanctuary is crowd control. In a small area such as Machias or the monarch preserve, visitors are in close contact with the protected animals. If those visitors are not limited in number and carefully controlled, the wildlife will suffer. Zones to buffer the preserve from the outside world are also critical. At Machias, the cold waters of the Gulf of Maine serve that purpose admirably. Bigger may be better for biodiversity, as predicted by island biogeography, but for some species, small works just fine.

Small would certainly have worked for the great auk. If some kind government—Iceland or Greenland or Canada—had protected just one island where it nested, the northern penguin would still be with us. And the size of the island protected wouldn't have made much difference.

CHAPTER 6

Goose Lake, Swan Lake
Mattamuskeet National Wildlife Refuge, North Carolina

As you drive east across the North Carolina coastal plain toward Lake Mattamuskeet, you will notice the towns getting smaller, the farms getting larger. In winter, many of the fields are brown with corn stubble and the disked remains of soybeans. But some are planted in winter wheat, and as you near the lake, you will begin to see great white splotches in those improbable emerald-green fields. By the time you reach Mattamuskeet National Wildlife Refuge, you may have identified the splotches. They are flocks of tundra swans, and their presence here is part of a puzzle that biologists are just beginning to solve—which is what brings me to the refuge today.

I park near a rusty gate. A sandy road overgrown with weeds leads into the refuge. The old road parallels Rose Bay Canal, a yardstick-straight ditch filled with black water. Loblolly pines line the road, dark green against a pale blue winter sky, and morning frost crunches beneath my boots. I pause to listen for waterfowl, but the air is still. Back in the early 1960s, you could hear the honking of Canada geese ten miles from the lake. But most of the geese are gone now, and the sound I'm hoping to hear is the softer calls of the birds that replaced them: tundra swans, *Cygnus columbiana*.

After a mile or so, the pines give way to waist-high yellow grasses. The *whoo-whoo*s of the swans are audible now. I've been here before, so I know that an impoundment lies around the next bend of the road. I slow my pace; swans are wary birds and will flee the impoundment if alarmed. A gray expanse of water opens in front of me. The swans' cries grow louder and more urgent. The flock nearest to me shifts restlessly on the water, and a dozen or so birds take flight, forming a scraggly, silvery V in the morning sun. I sink to the ground behind a tuft of tall grass and scan the impoundment with my binoculars. A hundred or more pale birds float on the water's surface. Gradually, they quiet down and resume their activities.

Tundra swans are large, all-white birds with six-foot wingspans. They breed in the far north, in Canada and Alaska, but great numbers of them winter at Mattamuskeet. Most of them rest and feed in the shallow, forty-thousand-acre lake for which the refuge is named, but I usually come to this small impoundment, where they are easier to observe. In either place, though—on the big lake or the impoundment—the swans appear very much at home, and most visitors are surprised to learn that they were not common at Mattamuskeet a few decades ago. The story of how they came to winter here involves one of the most fundamental concepts of ecology, and the decline of the Canada geese that they replaced illustrates an equally fundamental principle of wildlife management.

The tale begins in 1909, when the North Carolina Board of Education (which owned the property at the time) developed a plan to drain Mattamuskeet, the largest natural lake in North Carolina, to get at the rich soil of the lake bottom. The board of education, acting through the Mattamuskeet Drainage District, agreed to sell the lake—which was already famous for its wintering waterfowl—to the highest bidder. The drainage district and the buyer would share the cost of draining the lake, and the buyer would end up owning a sizable tract of cleared, virgin farmland. Almost fifty thousand acres were soon sold to a private company for two dollars per acre. Canals were dug and the largest pumping plant in the world installed. Then came the problems.

Cost overruns and heavy rains stalled the project, and two companies bankrupted themselves trying to drain the lake. Nevertheless, over twelve thousand acres of lake bed were in cultivation when the third owner, Augustus Hecksher, a wealthy New York businessman, shut down the unprofitable operation in 1932. Rain quickly refilled the lake, which Hecksher sold to the United States government two years later as a wildlife sanctuary. That year, a few thousand swans wintered at the new Mattamuskeet National Wildlife Refuge, but over twelve thousand Canada geese showed up.

By the winter of 1937, the goose population was up to 55,000, and the old pump house had been converted into a hunting lodge. Still, more geese came: 60,000 in 1940, 70,000 in 1950, and an astounding 131,100 in 1961. But swan populations didn't follow suit; in the big goose year of 1961, the swan count was a meager 930.

Why did geese come to Mattamuskeet in such numbers? Well, what do wintering geese need? The short answer is open water, safety from predators (including shotgun-toting humans), and food. The big lake, ringed by yummy marshes and partially protected from hunters (in the early days, goose hunting was permitted but carefully controlled), provided all three necessities. The long answer involves the ecological concept of *niche*.

Although the idea of ecological niches had been around for years, the word was first used to describe an animal's role in the environment by Charles Grinnell in a 1924 paper he wrote for the journal *Ecology*: "Some of us have concluded that we can usefully recognize, as measures of distributional behavior, the . . . ecologic or environmental niche. The latter, ultimate unit, is occupied by just one species or subspecies; if a new ecologic niche arises, or if a niche is vacated, nature hastens to supply an occupant, from whatever material may be available."

A few years later, the distinguished Oxford ecologist Charles Elton clarified Grinnell's definition. The niche of an animal, he wrote, "means its place in the biotic environment, its relations to food and enemies."

Niche is sometimes confused with habitat, but habitat corresponds to an animal's address, while niche refers to the part it plays in the habitat. Great blue herons and wood ducks, for example, are often found in the same freshwater ponds, but they play entirely different roles in that habitat. Herons feed primarily on fish and frogs. If their prey vanishes, so does their niche, and so do they. Wood ducks, on the other hand, eat aquatic vegetation, and as long as it is present, they will remain.

Of course, niches are not permanent. Nature and man regularly create and destroy them—which brings us back to geese. When rain refilled the Mattamuskeet lake bed, it created a vast new habitat with many vacant ecological niches, and as Grinnell predicted, "nature hastened to supply an occupant." In fact, lots of occupants were soon flourishing in the new lake: fish, frogs, and turtles; spike rush, bulrush, and wild millet; pintails, mallards, and many other species. Included in this immigration—this great niche filling—were thousands of Canada geese.

Now that the swans on the impoundment have settled down, I begin to sort out their activities. Some of them paddle about aimlessly—preening, calling to one another, and occasionally rising partially out of the water as they exercise their wings. But many float quietly on the surface of the impoundment, headless bundles of white feathers. These birds are feeding, often keeping their heads underwater for minutes at a time, stretching their long necks to graze the submerged vegetation that grows on the lake bottom.

As I watch, a dozen or more swans sail into the impoundment, braking with their wings before settling on the water. These swans have also been feeding, but not on aquatic plants. They have been scrounging in the farm fields that surround the lake, gleaning waste corn and soybeans and munching succulent shoots of winter wheat.

Although swans are new to field feeding, geese have been at it for centuries, plundering Egyptian wheat crops as long as three thousand years ago. When rain refilled Lake Mattamuskeet, Canada geese began wintering here to feed not only on the lake's sedges and grasses but also on farm crops.

Three distinct subpopulations of Canada geese ply the Atlantic flyway, each of which has its own breeding grounds. Historically, each subpopulation favored a particular wintering ground. But geese are sensible birds, and if they find ample food and open water north of their historic stopping places, some of them may spend the winter there. Many of the geese that poured into the new lake were probably birds that once wintered farther south.

After watching the swans on the impoundment for a while, my attention wanders, and I begin to notice other wildlife. Two red-tailed hawks soar over the pines on the far shore. A trio of white-tailed deer strolls casually into the water to feed on marsh grasses. Ducks swim around the margins of the lake, and egrets and great blue herons stand motionless in the shallow water.

Once, east of here, I saw an otter swimming in the black waters of a canal; a few minutes later, I spotted a peregrine falcon soaring overhead. Bears, weasels, and bobcats also roam this sanctuary, but those secretive creatures are hard to find. The Canada geese that once dominated the refuge—the birds that led sportsmen to name it the "Goose Hunting Capital of the World"—are also hard to find these days. Indeed, that is the mystery that brought me here: Why did swans wax and geese wane at Lake Mattamuskeet?

I walk back to my car and head for the refuge office. John Stanton, Mattamuskeet's resident biologist, has agreed to show me the lake's natural vegetation, the aquatic plants that swans and geese eat when they aren't feeding in fields. Perhaps the availability of natural foods altered the migration patterns of the two species.

I find John at his desk, a muscular, compact man with a trim mustache. His tiny office is packed with neat stacks of books and papers on waterfowl. Before John came to Mattamuskeet, he worked with waterfowl on a wildlife refuge in Louisiana. His master's degree is in wildlife biology; his thesis was about—what else?—waterfowl.

After a few minutes of polite conversation, John asks me if I'm ready to go. He slips on a pair of rubber boots and looks pointedly at my leather ones. "We usually find aquatic vegetation in the water."

"Well . . ."

"Never mind," he says. "I'll bring it to you on shore."

For the next hour, we slosh through mud and stands of brown and green marsh grasses. On higher ground, patches of tall plume grass sway in the breeze. Nearer the lake, the vegetation shrinks to waist height, then diminishes to a few inches in the shallow water. John finds samples of a sedge called Olney's three-square because of the distinctive triangular shape of its stems; he also finds wild millet and many more. I try to confirm John's identifications by looking in a field guide to aquatic plants that I've brought with me.

"Look at this," he says, pointing to a six-inch-tall tuft growing in the lake. "This is dwarf spike rush, *Eleocharis parvula*. It belongs to a category of plants called emergent vegetation. The roots are underwater, but the tops of the plants grow above the surface. Geese love this stuff."

John wades into deeper water. By now, my boots are soaked, so I wade out with him. He digs his hand into the mud at the bottom of the lake and brings up a gray-green plant. "Wild celery, *Vallisneria americanus*. This plant grows entirely beneath the water. It's a variety of SAV, submergent aquatic vegetation."

John digs into the lake again. He pulls out a handful of slimy stuff. "Muskgrass, another SAV," he says. "Don't bother trying to find it in your plant book—it's an alga. Swans use their long necks to graze on it and other SAV, which the geese can't reach."

In all, John finds nine plants and one alga important to geese or swans before I cry uncle. My hands are cold, my feet are cold, and I'm beginning to wonder if the mud will ever wash off.

Back in his office, I produce a list of plants that are important natural foods for geese. At the top of the list are spike rush, three-square, and millet. I show the list to John.

"Interesting," he says. "But these days, geese feed mostly in farm fields."

I produce another list and read from it. "On waste corn, soybeans, and shoots of winter wheat?"

"Yes," he says.

I think of the fields I passed this morning. "All of which are grown around here?"

"Yes."

"That leads to the $64,000 question," I say.

John leans back in his chair. "You want to know why we have so few geese here now?"

I find the census data John sent me earlier. "Over 144,000 geese wintered here in 1959. Last year, there were only a few thousand. The geese returned in numbers to fill an ecological niche that was created when the lake refilled. They needed the lake for resting and emergent vegetation and farm fields for feeding. All of those are still here, but where are the geese?"

John waves his hand. "Up there," he says. "On the Delmarva Peninsula. It's called shortstopping. Geese can get everything they need around Chesapeake Bay. Why waste energy flying farther south?"

"But they used to come here," I say. "Why did they stop?"

"I have some theories," John says slowly. "But in wildlife management, theories are a dime a dozen. Why don't you ask the refuge biologists on the Chesapeake? You might also want to talk to Kelly Davis. She had this job three years ago, when I came."

As I gather my notes to leave, John begins to file the reports he had laid out for our meeting. He is a careful, methodical man who prefers to stick to facts. In this, he resembles most wildlife biologists I have met. They are wary of speculations about *why* things happen in nature. Experience has shown them that nature is messy and theories often wrong. John is an intelligent man, and his ideas about the decline of geese at Mattamuskeet are probably as good as anyone's. But he's not about to go out on a limb for a doofus who wears leather boots to inspect aquatic vegetation.

To get some answers about why Mattamuskeet's geese began shortstopping, I take John's advice and call Keith Weaver, a wildlife biologist at Blackwater National Wildlife Refuge in Maryland.

After World War II, Keith says, farmers on the Delmarva Peninsula began switching from vegetable crops to cereal grains, mainly corn. They also started to plant winter wheat in the fall. As farmers grew more corn, they switched from highly efficient single-row harvesters to less efficient multi-row machines, which left more corn in the fields. The increasing availability of waste corn and winter wheat encouraged the geese to begin field feeding.

At the same time, northern refuges began to grow corn and millet specifically for geese. The refuge crops supplemented waste corn and winter wheat from nearby farms. These new food sources allowed more geese to winter on Chesapeake Bay and reduced the number of geese at Mattamuskeet—the once-proud "Goose Hunting Capital of the World"— to a few thousand birds.

About the time the geese began shortstopping, Keith adds, another change was taking place in the Chesapeake. Increased quantities of sediment and pollutants were destroying much of the bay's submerged aquatic vegetation. By the late 1960s, it was almost empty of SAV. But that didn't bother the geese; when they weren't field feeding on farms or at refuges, they could still find emergent vegetation, their preferred natural food.

In late September, I head back to Mattamuskeet. The corn in the fields has been cut, but the soybeans are still yellow-green, awaiting harvest. The lake is steel blue in the morning sunshine, the marshes verdurous. Near the causeway that bisects the lake, I spot a hundred or more Canada geese lounging in the shallows less than fifty feet from shore.

With their musical cries, long black necks, and white chin straps, Canada geese (*Branta canadensis*) are America's symbol of wildness. They remind us that wilderness lies just over the horizon, wilderness we may never see but know is there because of the presence of these birds. When I get out of the car, though, these geese don't rise into the air with alarm like wild birds. Instead, they drift sluggishly away from shore. These are summer geese, nonmigratory birds that spend their days grazing golf courses and office-park lawns. Humans are a normal part of their lives, and they are more familiar with water hazards than wilderness ponds.

In pre-European days, Canada geese nested almost exclusively—as one might expect—in Canada. Today, three-quarters of the Canada geese along the Atlantic flyway do not migrate at all in the conventional sense. They may move from one spot to another looking for better pickings, but they have never been to Canada and will never go there. The forebears of these birds were wing-clipped or pinioned when they were young, and they never learned to migrate. Some of the geese I see today are probably the descendants of birds that were once used as live decoys by commercial hunters, who released them when that practice was banned.

Kelly Davis greets me on the porch of her house, which sits just across the road from the refuge. Adjoining the house is a partially completed addition that dwarfs the original structure. Kelly has long, blond hair and a gracious smile. Despite being six months pregnant, she is wearing her usual outfit of jeans and T-shirt. When I first met Kelly, she was the wildlife biologist at Mattamuskeet, a job she held for fourteen years. These days, she is a wildlife consultant and does nature spots for a television show. She also keeps up with the local waterfowl scene, running wildlife tours for the refuge and talking regularly with John Stanton. Kelly Davis knows as much about Mattamuskeet's waterfowl as anyone.

We settle down to talk in her living room. I pull out my notes and begin. "First, some history. Geese have wintered at Mattamuskeet for centuries. As waste corn and winter wheat became available on the Delmarva Peninsula, the geese turned more and more to field feeding. This let them winter farther north, especially around Chesapeake Bay."

Kelly yawns and stretches. She's heard all of this before. "Right. But Dennis Luszcz over at the wildlife resources commission has some new ideas. Maybe shortstopping wasn't the only reason. You ought to call him."

I make a note to do that. "Okay," I continue. "Most tundra swans in the Atlantic flyway used to winter on Chesapeake Bay. Even after Mattamuskeet refilled, only a few thousand made it to the lake. We know the geese changed their migratory pattern to fill a vacant ecological niche at the new lake. Why didn't the swans change, too?"

"That's easy," Kelly says. "Swans and geese don't occupy identical niches, even though there's a lot of overlap. Swans prefer SAV. Geese like emergent vegetation. When Mattamuskeet refilled, emergent vegetation was plentiful. SAV wasn't."

"But John Stanton showed me huge beds of SAV—wild celery and muskgrass."

"You remember the old joke about the man who bragged about being the champion logger in the Sahara Forest?" she asks.

I do, so I feed her the next line. "The Sahara Forest? The Sahara's a desert."

Kelly smiles and provides the punch line. "'Yeah,' says the logger. 'Now.'"

"So SAV wasn't always plentiful at Mattamuskeet?"

"No. In fact, there was almost none in the early years. The lake was too turbid. Even though it's only two and one-half feet deep on average, not enough sunlight penetrated to support SAV."

"When did that change?"

Kelly leans forward on the couch, thinking. "Right after they removed the carp—in 1949, I think. Carp churned up the mud on the lake bottom. As soon as they were gone, the lake began to clear. Soon afterward, SAV appeared, mostly muskgrass. The refuge also sprigged wild celery and other aquatic plants. There's plenty of them, too."

The telephone rings, and while Kelly talks, I try to recall what I've read about the diet of wintering swans. I look through a book I've brought with me.

Frank Bellrose's *Ducks, Geese & Swans of North America* became the bible of North American wildlife managers after its publication in 1942. The 1976 edition lists tundra swans' winter diet at Chesapeake Bay. It includes wild celery and three other species of SAV. Bellrose further noted that in the winter of 1969, "swans departed from their long-standing tradition of feeding exclusively on aquatics and commenced a supplementary feeding on waste corn in fields on Maryland's Eastern Shore."

"Well," Kelly says, hanging up the telephone. "Did you find what you were looking for?"

"Yes. Bellrose confirmed what John Stanton told me; SAV is the food of choice for swans. So removing the carp allowed SAV to spread. That made Mattamuskeet swan heaven. But so was Chesapeake Bay. Why did they come down here?"

Kelly stands up. "I'm tired of sitting. Come see our addition." She takes me upstairs to the bedroom that she and her husband will occupy. Glass doors lead from the bedroom to a spacious deck. On it is a spotting scope. Less than fifty feet away are fields of corn and soybeans.

"These days, swans feed in the fields in the winter, just like geese have been doing for years," Kelly says. "This is a good place to watch them. Do you remember when swans started field feeding on the Delmarva Peninsula?"

"According to Bellrose, it was 1969."

"Do you know why?"

I recall Keith Weaver's comments. "Because pollution and sedimentation were killing off SAV in Chesapeake Bay. The geese didn't care; they were already field feeding, and they prefer emergent vegetation anyway."

"And that's why we have swans at Mattamuskeet," Kelly says trium-phantly. "Their numbers started to grow in the 1960s, as SAV dwindled in Chesapeake Bay. By 1990, we had forty-five thousand swans here."

I look out over the cornfields that make up Kelly's backyard. "But Bellrose said the swans were already field feeding on Delmarva. Why come south to feed in your fields?"

Kelly starts down the stairs. A German short-haired pointer races up to her and begins licking her hand. She scratches his ears absently. "Until recently, the swans fed in the lake before they went into the fields. They'd arrive at night from Chesapeake Bay and spend a week or two feeding on SAV. So SAV was still an important part of their diet back then. These days, though, they spend only a day or two on the lake before beginning to field feed. They're acting more and more like geese."

On my last trip to the refuge, I find Mattamuskeet gray and bleak in the waning light of a midwinter sun. A wavering skein of swans appears over the lake, passes almost overhead, then heads toward the fields of winter wheat. Though the total number of swans in the Mattamuskeet area is stable, John Stanton says the refuge population is down this year. Some of the swans have dispersed from the lake and established them-selves nearby. Nearly thirty thousand now winter at neighboring Pocosin Lakes National Wildlife Refuge, and another five thousand or so stay at Frying Pan, a bay of the Alligator River. John says that neither spot sup-ports much SAV and that both are too deep to graze. These swans have apparently abandoned their age-old winter feeding habits completely and now emulate geese by feeding almost exclusively in fields.

According to many North Carolina wildlife biologists, Dennis Luszcz knows more about the state's waterfowl than anyone. As waterfowl project leader for the North Carolina Wildlife Resources Commission, he has conducted banding projects and censuses throughout the state. Dennis thinks that more is going on with geese than just shortstopping. In a thoughtful letter to me on the subject, he said that shortstopping "is an oversimplification of what may be happening."

Back in the 1970s, Dennis began to suspect that the population of migratory geese in the Atlantic flyway was dropping, even though geese were plentiful up north. He believed that the decline in migratory geese was being masked in the northern states by an explosion in the number of nonmigrants—which are identical to migrants in appearance. His suspicions were confirmed in 1988, when biologists counted the geese at Ungava Bay in Quebec, a major breeding ground for the Atlantic flyway. The census showed fewer birds than expected.

In a 1996 article in *Wildlife in North Carolina*, Vic Venters summarized Luszcz's ideas and outlined a theory to explain the low number of geese in North Carolina (and at Mattamuskeet). It was called "differential survival." The theory was based on a common-sense premise—namely, that the birds that migrate the farthest are the most likely to be killed by hunters or die from natural causes. Thus, Mattamuskeet's migratory geese had a smaller chance of survival than those that wintered on Delmarva and at points north.

Since Mattamuskeet has only about 2,000 nonmigrant geese, the missing migrants left a big, easily detectable hole in the population. And as the number of geese dropped, the state began asking the Atlantic Flyway Council to set lower bag limits. But such concerns were pooh-poohed by the northern states, where geese were still plentiful. However, later surveys of the northern breeding grounds indicated that the number of migrant birds—low to begin with—was dropping, from about 120,000 pairs in 1988 to a low of 29,000 in 1995. That year, the council faced the issue and closed the hunting season on migratory geese along most of the Atlantic flyway. Today, goose season in North Carolina (and in other states along the flyway) starts and ends before migrant geese arrive.

The restrictions had an immediate impact on the breeding population at Ungava Bay. By the summer of 1997, the number of breeding pairs had doubled from the 1995 low. This effect has yet to be seen at Mattamuskeet, where midwinter counts are still minuscule. But finally, there is hope that the Canadas will return in greater numbers.

The breeding-ground data offers additional insight into the mystery that drew me to Mattamuskeet: Why did the swans wax and the geese wane? The following sequence of events answers most of the questions, but science is a work in progress, so even better answers may come along tomorrow.

1. Canada geese returned in numbers to Mattamuskeet to fill a vacant ecological niche when the lake refilled.

2. The decline in their population (by almost a factor of ten) between 1959 and 1967 was primarily due to shortstopping on the Delmarva Peninsula, where changes in agricultural practices made more food available to geese.

3. As the geese began shortstopping, SAV was on the decline in Chesapeake Bay. The dwindling SAV—the tundra swans' natural food—encouraged them to begin field feeding and moving farther south. They eventually arrived at Lake Mattamuskeet, where SAV was abundant.

4. As more winter wheat became available in the Mattamuskeet area, the swans began to feed in the fields, filling the ecological niche that the geese had vacated.

5. The continued decline of geese at Mattamuskeet over the last three decades was due in large part to overharvesting of migrant geese, a problem that was masked in the northern states by the increasing number of nonmigrant geese.

This chain of events illustrates once again the complicated nature of ecological problems. But once solved, the message from Mattamuskeet is a familiar one. It was expressed best by Kalli De Meyer, the manager of Bonaire Marine Park. She said that operating without research "is like trying to drive blindfolded." In this case, the wildlife managers at

Mattamuskeet were doing the research. They dutifully counted the geese and swans at the refuge every year and monitored the other populations along the Atlantic flyway; they were aware of the change in their feeding habits; and they constructed the shortstopping model to explain the data. Yet they were still driving blindfolded, their vision obscured by nonmigrant geese.

And as usual, without good data, politics prevailed. A lot of people—hunters, guides, manufacturers of hunting equipment—had an interest in keeping bag limits on geese high. It wasn't until the census data from the Canadian breeding grounds became available that wildlife managers had the information necessary to convince the Atlantic Flyway Council to restrict hunting seasons.

In *The Diversity of Life*, biologist E. O. Wilson of Harvard University offered several recommendations on what needs to be done to preserve global biodiversity. Number one on his list was finding out what's there. By this, he meant identifying all of the species that currently inhabit the planet. But Wilson also talked about the importance of counting the members of each species.

Just as politicians can't run a country without censuses, biologists cannot manage wildlife populations without them. And since wildlife doesn't respect man-made boundaries, only worldwide censuses will do. That notion sounds far-fetched, but if the wildlife managers along the Atlantic flyway had counted the breeding populations of geese in Canada earlier, the downward trend would have been apparent sooner and bag limits could have been reduced before the dangerously low numbers of geese at Ungava Bay were reached in 1995.

Good scientific data is hard to come by and is often expensive. The aerial surveys required for the Ungava Bay censuses are both. Nevertheless, they are necessary for good wildlife management. And once the censuses were started, progress followed. Today, migratory Canada geese are making a comeback on the Atlantic flyway.

The larger question posed by the events at Mattamuskeet is a critical one: Can we afford the Canadian censuses and others like them, as suggested by Wilson? As conservationists and ecologists from Henry David Thoreau to Aldo Leopold have observed, mankind is part of the web of life. If the web is unbroken and healthy, so are we.

If that is so, and I believe it is, then censuses are a small price to pay.

$\mathcal{W}$here the Buffalo Roam

Tallgrass Prarie Preserve, Oklahoma

THE CLOSEST TOWN to the Tallgrass Prairie Preserve is Pawhuska, Oklahoma, and the gathering spot in that town is the Bluestem Cafe. Long before seven in the morning, men in blue jeans, cowboy boots, and big, white hats sit at tables and talk about the weather or politics or cattle prices. The cafe is hazy with steam from coffee mugs and smoke from cigarettes. There is no bar, and beer signs do not adorn the walls. After years of eating in such places, I have formulated a theory about them: If smoking is allowed and drinking is not, then you are in the real country, the kind of place where the economy doesn't depend on boutiques or T-shirt shops. And Pawhuska is in the real country.

Pawhuska is the seat of Osage County, which lies on the Kansas border about fifty miles north of Tulsa. The county was named for the Osage Indians, who once dominated the region and whose tribal headquarters are still in Pawhuska. Royalties from oil pumped out of the wells sprinkled across Osage County—including over one hundred on the preserve itself—go to the tribe, which owns the mineral rights to all land in the county.

The northern part of the county is in the Flint Hills, a swath of rolling hummocks forty to seventy miles wide that stretches from northern Oklahoma across Kansas almost to Nebraska. Unlike most of the Midwest, deposits of limestone and chert lie beneath the surface of the Flint Hills, making the soil too shallow to plow. Consequently, the hills were spared the wheat and corn farming that prevail in much of the region. Today, oil and cattle dominate the economies of Osage County and the Flint Hills. The tallgrass prairie that once covered the hills has been grazed for a hundred years or more. Nevertheless, it is still a prairie landscape, rather than an agricultural one.

For that reason, when the 29,096-acre Barnard Ranch in the Oklahoma Flint Hills was offered for sale, The Nature Conservancy thought it would be a likely spot for a tallgrass preserve. It bought the property in 1989, and what has happened there since provides important lessons on how to create a nature reserve on land long used by humans.

Shortly after buying the land, The Nature Conservancy made some smart moves. The first was to hire a Pawhuska lawyer and photographer, Harvey Payne, as director. This soothed the anxieties of local ranchers, who were concerned about having a nature preserve run by outsiders. The second one was to bring in Bob Hamilton.

I meet Bob at a weathered picnic table behind the foreman's house at the preserve. He is a lean, muscular man in his late thirties, with a trim, brown mustache and an easy smile. He is wearing scuffed cowboy boots, faded jeans, and a dark blue T-shirt. A buffalo (or more correctly, a bison) is engraved on his oversized belt buckle. Bob's title is science director of the Tallgrass Prairie Preserve, but he looks more like a cowboy than a scientist. As it turns out, he is both—a good scientist and a man of the plains.

Bob grew up in small-town Kansas, where he worked on farms and ranches in the summer. He went to undergraduate and graduate school in Kansas, earning degrees in environmental biology. He started with The

Nature Conservancy in 1982, working on preserves in the Dakota plains. Today, he is the second-in-command for one of the conservancy's most ambitious projects—the restoration of the tallgrass prairie on land that was once a cattle ranch.

"The Flint Hills," he tells me, "is about all that's left of the tallgrass prairie. Although most of it is being ranched, it is still a native-plant-dominated system of grasses and forbs, which is a heck of a lot better than soybeans or a subdivision.

"What was missing here were the disturbances you got on the original prairie. Our idea was to restore—as best we could—the original disturbance regime. The historical reviews we did showed that bison were the primary grazers. The other missing element was fire—random fire. Now, we've restarted the engine, and we'll just see where it goes. In a sense, we're just following along behind to see what happens."

One glance at the land I can see from the picnic table tells me that the engine is going in the right direction. Beyond the oaks that shade us from the September sun is rolling prairie, mile after mile of waist-high brown and green grasses sprinkled with wildflowers. Other than the trees we are sitting under, there is nothing taller than a man's head between us and the horizon. Although it's hard to believe, this prairie was once forested. And the event that leveled that forest happened millions of years ago and hundreds of miles away.

The Rocky Mountains lie five hundred miles west of the Flint Hills. They rose during the Laramide orogeny. Geologists are still arguing about the nature of that event and exactly when it occurred. However, most of them agree that the Rockies were in place about 25 million years ago. Then as now, the prevailing winds across North America were westerlies. When the moist air coming off the Pacific Ocean encountered the western mountains, it rose. The cooler temperatures of the higher elevations condensed the moisture, which fell as rain or snow on the mountains and produced a rain shadow to the east. That rain shadow started a 25-million-year drought that killed the forests and created the grasslands that we now call the Great Plains. Since then, those grasslands have waxed and waned as the climate changed, but they have never vanished.

North American grasslands exist where precipitation is between ten and forty inches per year. Less than ten is desert; more than forty is forest. The amount of precipitation also determines the height of the grasses. The driest grasslands, those closest to the moisture draining Rockies, are shortgrass prairies. Next come the mixed-grass prairies. And the easternmost plains, the wettest of the three thanks to moisture-laden breezes from the Gulf of Mexico, produce tallgrass prairies—or as they are sometimes called, true prairies. The true prairies once covered 140 million acres from Canada to Texas, from Indiana to Kansas. The Flint Hills of Kansas and northern Oklahoma were part of that great expanse of tallgrass.

Grasses and forbs (a group of broad-leaved plants that includes many wildflowers) thrive in drier climates than trees can tolerate because of their deep, spreading roots, which trap and absorb moisture efficiently, and their small leaves, which minimize the evaporation of water. Big bluestem (*Andropogon gerardi*), a major component of the tallgrass prairie, has a dense web of roots that can extend ten or more feet into the soil. Although big bluestem can reach heights exceeding six feet, most of the plant is below ground. This is true of other prairie grasses and forbs, too. The extensive roots of these plants make them resistant to drought; they also enable the grasses and forbs to survive the herbivores that graze on them.

When the Rockies' rain shadow converted the plains from forests to grasslands, the great buffet of grasses opened new ecological niches for herbivores. One of the first grazers on the new grasslands was a small, leaf-eating ancestor of the modern horse called miohippus, whose fossils provided a clue that helped date the Laramide orogeny. About 25 million years ago, its teeth began to elongate, an adaptation that paleontologists believe occurred when it began eating tough prairie grasses. Miohippus was joined on the early plains by New World camels and other grazers.

The number of species on the plains swelled during the ice ages of the Pleistocene epoch (which began about 1.8 million years ago), when Eurasian animals ventured across the newly exposed Beringian land bridge. Among them were the first bison to reach North America.

The Eurasian steppe bison (*Bison priscus*), a huge animal that was half again larger than modern bison, crossed Beringia and entered Alaska over seventy thousand years ago. We know these creatures not only from their bones but also from images painted on the limestone walls of the caves at Lascaux, France, and other sites. One famous drawing depicts two massive, hump-shouldered bison with surprisingly gracile hindquarters facing away from each other. Although the Neolithic artist gave one figure an impressionistic red eye, their resemblance to today's North American bison is striking and unmistakable.

B. priscus never made it to the Great Plains, but two of its descendants migrated south—the long-horned, now-extinct *B. latifrons* and *B. bison*, the modern plains bison. Cowboys called *B. bison* the buffalo, but it is only distantly related to the true buffalo of India and Africa. Still, the old-timers' name persists thanks to another famous image—the engraved bull on the buffalo nickel.

In presettlement days, between 30 million and 60 million bison roamed the Great Plains. They comprised half of what Bob Hamilton called the prairie's "original disturbance regime." Their demise (and the demise of the Indians who depended on them) has been told over and again. And it was in fact a brutal slaughter. In less than two decades, commercial hunters almost wiped out North American bison, most of which were skinned and left to rot on the prairie, while Indians starved or were herded on to reservations. Fewer than a thousand bison were left when the killing stopped, almost all of them in zoos or preserves.

On that new prairie—now bisonless and "civilized"—European settlers altered the other half of the ancient disturbance regime: the pattern of fires that had been in place for millennia.

⁙

The earliest prairie fires were started by lightning. In her book, *Big Bluestem*, Annick Smith checked the records of the United States Weather Service, which reported that the Flint Hills drew the second-highest number of lightning strikes in the country. (The highest number is usually recorded in Florida, where periodic fires helped create that state's longleaf-pine savannas.) There is little doubt that the frequency of fires picked up when the first humans arrived on the prairies about eleven thousand years ago. According to Lewis and Clark, Indians set fires to improve the quality of grass "as an inducement for the Buffalow to feed."

Regardless of how they were ignited, prairie fires in the tallgrass were awesome events. Driven by strong winds, encouraged by drought and heat, and fueled by tinder-dry vegetation, walls of flame five miles long and thirty feet high roared across the prairies. In her book, *Grasslands*, Lauren Brown quoted a Methodist circuit rider who saw such a fire one night in 1835: "By the light of this fire we could read fine print for ½ a mile or more."

Surprisingly, such conflagrations do little permanent damage to the vegetation of the tallgrass prairie. Despite temperatures that can exceed a thousand degrees Fahrenheit, a fast-moving prairie fire barely heats the soil below the surface. Thus, the deep and extensive root systems of the grasses and forbs are undamaged by even the hottest blazes. In fact, according to a 1993 report in the journal *American Midland Naturalist*, properly timed burns can significantly stimulate the growth of big bluestem.

Most of the early settlers didn't care about the beneficial effects of fires. They were raising corn, wheat, and children. Wildfires endangered their crops and their families. Fire suppression became the order of the day. Even in the Flint Hills, where cattle ranching prevailed and ranchers were thoroughly familiar with the fertilizing effects of fire, they restricted their burnings to the spring. The summer and cool-season fires that had historically been part of the natural prairie were lost.

The change in fire regime combined with cattle grazing to alter the ecology of the Flint Hills—the complex interaction among plants, fire, and bison that began in the Pleistocene. Over the years, virtually every scrap of the great North American tallgrass prairie was either plowed under or converted for cattle ranching. The job facing The Nature Conservancy when it bought the Barnard Ranch was to restore the natural forces that created the original tallgrass prairie.

⤳

Bob Hamilton wades through the waist-high vegetation of the prairie, pointing out the different species. "First, the Big Four." He shows me big bluestem, a tall perennial grass with stiff, dry leaves that often dominates the tallgrass prairie; bunches of little bluestem, a tan-colored plant at this time of year; Indian grass, which has tall, golden seed heads; and switch grass, a medium-height, yellow-green panic grass with curly leaves and delicate seed heads that sway in the breeze.

Then he picks up the pace of his delivery. "Purpletop," he intones. "Missouri goldenrod, native thistles, lance-leafed ragweed, and dewberry."

Every plant on the prairie seems to be a different species, and I soon give up trying to write down the names.

"These are only a few," Bob says. "There's over seven hundred total plant species in the preserve."

"So is this the presettlement landscape? Is this what it looked like?"

"Who knows?" he says, striding easily through the grass. "I get that question all the time. We looked back in history to get an idea of how things worked, but those are incomplete pictures. Our gauge of success out here is not going to be whether we have re-created the past, but an analysis of how well we maintain native biotic diversity."

It is clear that Bob Hamilton has thought deeply about restoration ecology, combining his scientific education with years of practical experience on the prairie to develop some hard-won ideas. Although restoration ecology is a new field, many ecologists believe it is our best hope for reclaiming degraded ecosystems.

The new discipline recently got an important stamp of approval. In a 1998 speech at the annual conference of the Ecological Society of America, Secretary of the Interior Bruce Babbitt predicted great things for the new discipline: "The twentieth century was dominated by the concept of preservation; the twenty-first will be dominated by the concept of restoration."

But exactly what is this concept that the secretary believes will be so important in the coming century? In one ecology text, Begon, Harper, and Townsend defined restoration ecology as "the science concerned with the deliberate colonization and revegetation of derelict land." The definition seems incomplete. Colonization and revegetation by what? And to what end? Those are the questions that Bob Hamilton must answer every day.

One question that has been answered about this nascent science is where best to practice it. Prairies appear to be ideal. Stephen Packard and Cornelia Mutel made that point in *The Tallgrass Restoration Handbook*. Prairies, they wrote, "lend themselves to restoration" because they "are amenable to tinkering on a reasonable scale and over a reasonable period of time. Many prairie plants mature fairly rapidly. In fact, most will flower and set seed within five years." That fast maturation is indeed a plus; restoring an old-growth forest could take five centuries or more.

Actually, what Bob Hamilton is doing on the old Barnard Ranch is more rehabilitation than restoration. Most, and perhaps all, of the native plants were present when he began his work. A big part of his job today is managing the two missing elements that The Nature Conservancy has reintroduced: bison and fire.

Prairie fires are not new in Osage County; most ranchers burn every spring to stimulate the growth of new grass, as their predecessors did for a hundred years or more before them. But Bob Hamilton's fire regime is different. He randomly selects when and where to burn. This, he believes, better mimics the historic pattern—or lack of pattern—of prairie fires in the Flint Hills. He conducts thirty or more burns each year, and he has a hangar-sized building full of equipment to help start and control them. Flame-resistant suits hang from hooks, and all-terrain vehicles sit beside two large yellow trucks with hoses and gauges, one of which is known as "Daisy."

"When we first bought this place, we began by conducting ecological surveys," Bob says. "Since we didn't burn during that period, we built up a lot of fuel. That concerned our neighbors. They said 'You have thirty-something thousand acres out here just ready to explode. What are you going to do about it?'

"I had a similar problem when I was managing Cross Ranch Preserve up north of Bismarck. Nobody knows who you are. You know, 'The Nature Conspiracy's coming to town.' Everybody assumes that we're the big, bad eastern environmental organization. That we're going to kick butt and take names. You can talk about being good guys, but they want to see you do it. Walk the walk. Make sure we aren't selling flowers at the airport or being real goofy."

The idea of Bob Hamilton selling flowers at the airport—or anywhere else—strikes me as preposterous. "You, selling flowers?"

It must strike him as preposterous, too, because he laughs. "Anyway, we geared up to suppress wildfires," he continues. "In October and November, you can really get some screamers. The fuel is all standing there nice and fluffy and cured. You get those Indian summer days, eighty degrees, thirty-mile-an-hour south wind. What they say around here is 'That one's going to Topeka.' And theoretically, it could. It just rocks and rolls.

"So we really took an active role. We've chased about three dozen fires on our neighbors' properties in the last five or six years. I think we've established ourselves as responsible neighbors—but it took awhile. These days, when our program calls for a fire, we often do joint burns with our neighbors."

The Tallgrass Prairie Preserve has thrived under the random-fire regime. The land is a mosaic of healthy grasses and forbs interspersed with black, burned patches dusted with light green shoots. On neighboring cattle ranches, the grasses are shorter and browner and more uniform, more like a meadow than a prairie.

The fires also hold back the trees. In the Flint Hills, which lie in the eastern, moister part of the Great Plains, trees constantly invade the prairie. Without fires, much of the Flint Hills would become forest. In borderline prairies like this, both fires and aridity are necessary to maintain grasslands. Bob Hamilton's controlled burns merely continue the tradition the Indians started centuries ago of maintaining this prairie by fire.

Burning benefits the bison, too. Most of the bison I saw were feeding on new, tender shoots of green in the burned areas. "Sucking ash," Bob Hamilton calls it.

The question is, Have the bison benefited the prairie? If they haven't, why not run cattle like everyone else?

The bison is the largest land animal in North America. A full-grown male can stand six feet tall at the shoulder and weigh a ton. They are fierce-looking beasts, especially in their shaggy winter coats. But their appearance belies their true nature; bison are generally docile creatures, more closely related to cows than to the more unpredictable and dangerous true buffalo. In fact, a move is afoot to change their scientific name from *Bison* to *Bos*, which would place them in the same genus as cows.

Similar though they are, cattle and bison differ in their grazing habits on the prairie. About a quarter of cows' intake is forbs, while bison shun forbs and feed almost exclusively on grass. Thus, replacing cows with bison tends to promote the growth of forbs. And since there are far more species of forbs than grasses in the tallgrass prairie, bison tend to promote biodiversity. Today, many of the plants in the preserve are forbs, and many of the forbs are wildflowers.

Although Bob Hamilton is not trying to reproduce the presettlement prairie, reintroducing fire and bison appear to be moving the preserve in that direction. Wildflowers—goldenrod, compass plant, and many others—brighten the Tallgrass Prairie Preserve. Wildflowers were also rampant on the presettlement prairie. D. D. Owens described the scene in 1848: "On the summit levels spreads the wide prairie, decked with flowers of the gayest hue" (Kline 1997).

Bob Hamilton appreciates the beauty of flowers, but as a scientist, he also appreciates how forbs foster biodiversity. "Diversity builds on itself," he tells me when we resume our interview. "There are a few invertebrates that are obligates on grass." An obligate is a species that depends on another species to survive; the monarch butterfly, for example, is an obligate of milkweed. "But there's much more of that going on with the forbs. So the assumption is that as your plant community gets more forb species, that will build the insect community. The greater seed supply should build the small-mammal community. And so forth. This biotic diversity, which the bison foster, is one of our major goals. The result may resemble the presettlement tallgrass prairie, but some of the pieces are still missing—and some of them will probably always be missing."

"Wolves and grizzlies?"

"Yeah. And there's no way to bring them back. After all, this is cow country, and we can't introduce big predators. We already have a healthy coyote population, and we're probably going to leave it at that. The other big missing species is elk. In this part of the plains—the eastern part—elk were a major player. Pronghorn were also here, but in much lower numbers."

"Are you bringing back elk?"

Bob looks out over the prairie. His eyes follow a rooster tail of dust rising behind a pickup speeding along the preserve's main road. I hear a wistful note in his voice. "Maybe at some point in the future . . ."

I've spent so much time at the Bluestem Cafe that when I arrive there early one morning, the waitress greets me with a question. "The usual?" she asks, filling my coffee cup.

I nod.

Minutes later, she places a platter overflowing with eggs, bacon, and homemade biscuits covered with white gravy in front of me. "Going out to the preserve again?" she asks.

"Yep. Got to process this cholesterol."

"I've never been there, but it's supposed to be pretty. Watch out for the buffalo, though. People run into them all the time."

An hour later, I am sitting in my car in the middle of two dozen or so bison. Directly in front of me is a huge bull, head lowered. An old Roger Miller song comes to mind: "You Can't Roller Skate in a Buffalo Herd." Nor, I think, can you drive in one.

After the bison's brush with extinction, herds were rebuilt in preserves in the United States and Canada. Their descendants make up the Tallgrass Prairie Preserve's herd. It was started with three hundred bison donated by Kenneth and Diana Adams in 1993. Today, nearly eight hundred bison roam the eighty-six-hundred-acre bison unit. In the next five years, the herd is expected to grow to twenty-two hundred head that will be able to move freely over the entire preserve. Today, though, the land outside the bison unit is fenced off and leased out for cattle grazing; the money from these leases and from the annual culling of the bison herd helps defray the preserve's operating expenses. But there are no fences inside the unit, and the bison are free to roam wherever they choose.

Today, they choose the road. The bull in front of me moves languidly to the shoulder, munches a tuft of grass, then leaps nimbly over a ditch and wanders out on to the prairie. I edge forward. As soon as I am free of the bison, I gun it. I plan to see the prairie up close today.

I start the preserve's three-mile nature trail on a cool, sunny morning. The path begins in the bottom land along Sand Creek and winds through a ten-foot-tall patch of big bluestem. A gallery forest of oaks and ashes and redbuds lines the stream. Three white-tailed deer burst from the forest, then stop to stare at me before hightailing it back into the woods. After passing an upland forest of blackjack oaks, the trail breaks out on to the prairie.

From a distance, the prairie appears to be a gold-green monoculture, but up close, it is a confusing array of plants. I recognize big and little bluestem, goldenrod, and some of the other common plants that Bob Hamilton showed me. But most species I can't identify. Some are tall; others are short. Some are brown; others are green. A few are in flower; most are not. Bob Hamilton said that over seven hundred species of plants grow in the preserve, and this trail transforms that number into bewildering reality. And for someone who likes to name plants as he walks, that reality is overwhelming. So I give up and try to take in the rest of what the prairie has to offer.

Brightly colored butterflies flit from one purple-flowered thistle to another. Cicadas and grasshoppers spring into the air beside the trail. Cryptic brown moths whiz by my head. Vultures circle above the trail, and piles of coyote scat sit in the middle of it. Mourning doves whistle into the air when my footsteps flush them, and three killdeer peck away in a burned patch. The birds that interest me the most, however, are the hawks.

I've already spotted red-tails in the trees and kestrels on utility wires beside the road, but the most common hawks on the prairie are northern harriers. They sail low over the ground, dipping and twisting a few feet above the tallgrass. When they spot something that interests them, they flutter for a moment, then stoop. I see one rise from the ground with what looks like a mouse in its talons.

I remember Bob Hamilton's words: "Diversity builds on itself." Clearly, that is happening on the preserve. From plants to invertebrates, from small mammals to birds to larger animals, this prairie is filled with life. And a walk through the tallgrass showcases its diversity.

During my last session with Bob, he tells me about threats to the preserve. "What's really popped up here in the last few years is exotic-plant problems. The big nine-hundred-pound gorilla that's showed up is a forb, *Lespedeza cuneata*. It's from East Asia, I think. It's a real problem throughout the Flint Hills. It showed up in Kansas back in the mid-1980s, and it's just ballooned. I think they have three hundred thousand acres now infested in Kansas. It has fairly low palatability, too. Cattle will take it early in the growing season, but it builds up tannins, and it's not palatable by midsummer.

"Our bison can't help us with this problem; they consume less than 1 percent forbs. So we've started spraying. I guess this is the third year of spot treatments. And we're still not over the hump."

He turns to face me, and a sly smile replaces the serious expression. "Who knows?" he says. "Maybe if we brought the elk back, they'd be lespedeza eaters."

Probably, though, the elk wouldn't do the trick. And that leaves people. At the Tallgrass Prairie Preserve, nature is clearly managed. The spraying, the burning, and the annual roundup of bison to cull the fast-growing herd fly in the face of some commonly held notions about what a "nature preserve" should be.

Some preservationists believe that people shouldn't meddle with nature in a preserve, that nature should make the rules. You create preserves, their theory goes, by finding pristine, or almost pristine, wilderness, which you fence off from the rest of the world, then allow nature to take its course. Most of the United States' great national parks were created that way. In fact, the park service's mandate—"To conserve the scenery and the natural and historic objects and the wildlife therein"—does not mention managing the land. Similarly, the Wilderness Act of 1964 specifies that a wilderness area must "retain its primeval character and influence, without permanent improvement or human habitation."

Both parks and wilderness areas play important roles in preserving wildlife. But few parks or wilderness areas—maybe none—are big enough to exist without human help on occasion. In his book, *Playing God in Yellowstone*, Alston Chase made the argument for active management of nature preserves: "Western civilization has radically altered these places, which were never complete ecosystems, and they remain as tiny islands surrounded by technological society. The eviction of Indians, elimination of predators, introduction of exotic species of plants and animals have thrown even the 'wildest' parks into ecologic disequilibrium."

Some of the opposition to active management comes from a few environmental groups that believe that the managers themselves are the problem. They prefer no management to what they feel is incompetent management. (The next chapter, "The Antelope Dilemma," gives one example of such a group.) These folks have many stories to back them up. The classic one, the one that environmental Luddites most often trot out, involves the United States government's attempts at predator control.

The elimination of predators has been an official policy of our government for most of its history. That misguided policy produced catastrophic results. When mountain lions and wolves were eliminated from the Kaibab Plateau in Arizona in the 1920s, deer populations first soared, then—with no predators to restrain their numbers—crashed as the herds ate all of the available forage and starved. The story became known as the "lesson of the Kaibab" and was recounted beautifully by Aldo Leopold in *A Sand County Almanac*.

Mistakes like that have made some people understandably chary of human intervention in natural processes. I believe that to be a shortsighted view. In ecology—as in any science—mistakes are made; that's one way science progresses. The Industrial Revolution badly polluted the air of Great Britain. The solution, though, was not to shut down the machines, but to clean up the emissions. And today, even the most militant environmentalists wear clothes produced on latter-day versions of the textile equipment that the original Luddites tried to destroy.

The Tallgrass Prairie Preserve—now grown to 38,600 acres—is by any standard a success for restoration ecology. A cattle ranch has been transformed into a biologically diverse tallgrass prairie. Ironically, it takes a lot of human intervention to allow the natural forces that originally shaped the ecosystem to continue to operate. But that is a price our society has been—and hopefully will continue to be—willing to pay.

Don't be fooled, though. The price is high. Expensive humans have replaced the grizzlies and wolves that once culled the bison herds for nothing, and costly equipment is required to control wildfires that once raced freely across the prairie. But the money and intervention have paid off. Over twenty thousand people visited the preserve last year.

When I meet a young woman from Tulsa in the preserve's gift shop, I ask her why she has come here. She says she has lived in Oklahoma all her life and that she wants "to see what the state used to look like."

I consider telling her that the goal here isn't to re-create the past but to enhance biotic diversity. However, pursuing the latter seems to have led to the former, so I keep my mouth shut.

CHAPTER 8

The Antelope Dilemma

Hart Mountain National Antelope Refuge, Oregon

I CRUISE SLOWLY along the gravel road that leads north from the Hart Mountain visitor center. It is a warm late-summer day, and the resinous smell of sagebrush blows in through the open windows of the car. In every direction is typical high-desert terrain, an open range of yellow grasses and low-lying forbs spotted with gray-green clumps of big sage. The land is as flat as a Kansas cornfield, except for low, brown hills on the horizon. In the distance, dark specks pick their way across the golden prairie.

About a mile farther north, five of those dark specks are close enough to the road for me to see them clearly. They are pronghorns, the sleek buff-and-white antelopes for which this refuge was named. When I get out of the car to watch them through my binoculars, they freeze and stare at me as curiously as I am staring at them.

After a minute or two of mutual gawking, the pronghorns—a buck and four does—begin to move restlessly. Two of them run a short distance this way, then another pair runs a short distance that way. Then they stop and mill around nervously. Finally, the group reaches a consensus, and they all hightail it across the open prairie, running smoothly and effortlessly through the grass before disappearing in the distance.

As I watch them fade away, another lean, brown form lopes across the road only fifty yards from me. The coyote traces a haphazard route through the sagebrush, sniffing here, then there, always moving, tail low to the ground.

Within minutes of my arrival, I have seen both of the animals that brought me here. These sightings are not unusual; both pronghorns and coyotes are common on this refuge. But the way they interact here at Hart Mountain is unusual. The two species are engaged in a war, which the coyotes are winning. And we humans may have inadvertently shifted the odds in their favor.

The key word in the previous sentence is *may*. No one knows for sure what the natural balance between the two species is or how that balance oscillates over time. And that poses a dilemma for the refuge's managers. Should they intervene in this war, or should they let nature take its course? How that question is answered goes to the heart of what national wildlife refuges are all about.

To understand this dilemma better, we must learn more about the actors in the drama. And as we shall see, both of them have occupied this territory for quite a while.

The pronghorn (*Antilocapra americana*) is the only surviving species of a once-diverse family of ruminants, or cud chewers, that roamed North America as early as 20 million years ago. Much about its scientific name is confusing. *Antilocapra americana* means, literally, "American goat-antelope," but only one-third of that name is accurate. Pronghorns—which are often called antelopes—are American, but they are unrelated to the true antelopes of the Old World, examples of which are the gazelles and impalas of Africa. Nor are they closely related to goats, which belong to another group of ungulates called bovines.

However, the name *pronghorn* fits perfectly; bucks do sport horns with a single prong. So if some stickler for nomenclatural accuracy is ever assigned the chore of renaming North American wildlife sanctuaries, then Hart Mountain National Antelope Refuge will undoubtedly become Hart Mountain National *Pronghorn* Refuge. Most Americans, however, use the names *antelope* and *pronghorn* interchangeably, a practice I will follow throughout this chapter.

The Pleistocene epoch, which started about 1.8 million years ago, brought great climate changes to North America. Glaciers expanded and contracted, grasslands came and went, and the first humans crossed the Beringian land bridge to the continent. When the upheavals of that epoch ended 10,000 years ago, only one of the many pronghorn-like species that had once roamed the continent's grasslands was left, *A. americana*. But what modern pronghorns lacked in diversity, they made up for in numbers.

The Lewis and Clark expedition provided one of the first written reports of pronghorns, which the men called "goats." They spotted them first in September 1804, as the expedition headed up the Missouri River. The men pointed out one to Meriwether Lewis shortly after they entered the shortgrass prairie near today's Nebraska–South Dakota border. According to Lewis biographer Stephen Ambrose, Lewis later "saw more wild goats on a hill, but they ran off before he could even describe their color." Eleven days later, Captain William Clark killed one of the mysterious goats, which Sergeant John Ordway, employing the whimsical spelling and punctuation common in those days, described in his journal: "Capt Clark . . . killed a curious annimil resembling a Goat. . . . It was 3 feet high . . . the legs like a Deer: feet like a goat. horns like a Goat only forked . . . hair thick & of white and dark reddish collour. Such an animal was never yet known in U.S. States."

The pronghorns' curious appearance did not deter the expedition from enjoying antelope steaks. Lewis and Clark's men killed, and presumably ate, sixty-five of them during their journey. The antelopes were easy pickings; according to every account, the prairies swarmed with pronghorns. Estimates of their number vary, but most scientists today believe that 30 million to 60 million antelopes grazed the North American grasslands before white settlers arrived, a population of large mammals second only to the bison. John Byers, who conducted years of pronghorn research on the National Bison Range in Montana, set the number at 50 million, and that figure is probably as good as any.

Pronghorns ranged widely across the West from southern Canada to northern Mexico. Their greatest concentration, however, was on the short-grass prairies of the Great Plains. Fewer were found west of the Rockies. And one of the westernmost populations grazed the shrubby steppes of the Great Basin in western Nevada and south-central Oregon.

As farms replaced open prairie, pronghorn habitat was lost. Where it was too dry to farm, pronghorns had to compete with cattle. And in both cases, the fences erected by settlers drove pronghorns crazy.

Unlike its distant cousin the white-tailed deer, which can clear a five-foot barrier with ease, the pronghorn rarely jumps over fences. It usually tries to crawl under them or through them. The mere sight of a fence can panic a pronghorn. Byers noted that when mothers get separated from their fawns by a fence, "the pair may spend hours or days frantically running back and forth before one manages to cross." Even when a fence is removed, antelopes sometimes seem confused and act as though it were still in place. Because pronghorns move from one range to another to find forage, the fencing of the West was bad news for them.

Almost as bad as the fences was unrestrained hunting. Hungry settlers with long-range rifles replaced Indians with bows and arrows. Market hunting was common, and millions of pronghorns were converted into savory roasts in the burgeoning cities of the United States.

The demise of the great antelope herds eerily paralleled that of the bison. By the early twentieth century, the pronghorn population had dropped to thirteen thousand. In less than one hundred years, over 99.9 percent of the world's pronghorns were gone. Once again, humans had proved themselves the most efficient predator ever to appear on the planet.

Fortunately, by the turn of the century, some people were beginning to grasp that fact and push for laws to protect wildlife. Conservationists of the day demanded an end to antelope hunting, and the western states responded. North Dakota banned it in 1899, Montana in 1903, and Wyoming in 1909. By 1920, wolves, the other main predators of pronghorns, were also waning. The decline of wolves and hunting halted the pronghorns' slide toward extinction, and populations, although still low, began to stabilize.

Meanwhile, the government was waging war against another pronghorn predator. But its campaign would prove unsuccessful. Humans may be the most efficient predators on the planet, but coyotes have thrived despite our attempts to wipe them out.

Like pronghorns, coyotes (*Canis latrans*) have been around for a long time. They are members of the Canidae, or dog, family. Some branches of this family evolved into huge creatures the size of bears. The dire wolf of the Pleistocene is an example. Those fearsome animals are now extinct, but the smaller, more adaptable members of the family flourished. In North America, species of the genus *Canis* arose two to four million years ago. From them came today's foxes, wolves, and coyotes.

Although the modern coyote resembles its big brother the wolf, scientists believe the coyote is more closely related to the fox. Coyotes are closer in size to foxes than they are to wolves. They have narrow skulls like foxes and weak jaws that lack the grasping power to bring down the large game—such as antelopes and elk—favored by wolves. Coyote teeth have large chewing surfaces, which are suitable in a pinch for munching vegetation and are less specialized than the teeth of the almost exclusively carnivorous wolves. These differences made coyotes more adaptable to humans than were wolves. It also dictated how they prey on pronghorns. Because adults are too big and too fast to bring down, the ever-adaptable coyotes learned to concentrate on fawns.

As with pronghorns, the first Americans to encounter coyotes were members of the Lewis and Clark expedition. On August 12, 1804, an animal that Clark called a "Prairie Wolf" barked at their boat as they made their way up the Missouri. The men of the expedition reacted to the coyote in the same way that most Americans who followed them west would; they went ashore to kill it. Clark reported, "We could not git him," a result that foreshadowed what was to come.

In the century that followed the Lewis and Clark expedition, coyotes were considered pests by almost everyone in the West. In the 1840s, Audubon summarized the prevailing attitude toward coyotes in his *Viviparous Quadrupeds of North America*: "By its predatory and destructive habits, this Wolf is a great annoyance to the settlers in the new territories of the west. Travellers and hunters on the prairies, dislike it for killing the deer, which supply these wanderers with their best meals." As a matter of course, most sheepherders and cattle ranchers shot coyotes on sight. But for the coyotes, the worst was yet to come.

Early settlers tried bounties to eliminate predators. The first bounty in North America was placed on wolves in 1630, less than a decade after the Pilgrims landed at Plymouth Rock; the Massachusetts Bay Company paid one penny per wolf. Other colonies soon followed suit. By 1800, the wolves in New England were largely gone.

But the bounty system didn't work as well in the West. Iowa, for example, offered a two-dollar bounty on wolves and coyotes in 1795. Although wolves were depleted, both species were still present in the state a hundred years later. Bounty hunting was equally ineffective in other western states. So loud were the howls of stockmen who continued to lose sheep and cattle to predators that the federal government finally took action.

In 1915, Congress established the agency that became Animal Damage Control, an organization that exists to this day. The idea was to provide stockmen with professional help in exterminating coyotes and other predators, including wolves, cougars, bobcats, and anything else that

threatened sheep and cattle. The professionals didn't just shoot predators; they trapped them, gassed them, and poisoned them, too. The black-
and-white photographs of the day told the story: piles of cougar heads,
dead coyote pups laid out near their den, a snarling wolf with one foot
caught in a steel trap. By 1930, the wolf was almost completely extirpated from the United States. (Robust populations still roamed Alaska,
but it didn't become a state until 1959.) One writer, Mark Derr, estimated that over four million coyotes have been killed since A.D.C. was
established.

But the coyote refused to go the way of the wolf. Wolves usually
prey on large animals; after the bison and antelope herds were decimated,
their primary targets were cows. This brought them into often-lethal contact with humans. But coyotes prefer smaller game. They are shy and
secretive, less specialized and more adaptable than wolves. Although the
government's intensive warfare did reduce coyote populations in some
areas, the species hung on and even managed to expand its range.

One of the places where coyotes persisted was the Great Basin, where
a remnant of the great herds of antelopes still survived.

To the east are the Rockies, to the west the Cascade (or Sierra) Mountains. To the north is the Columbia Plateau, to the south the Mojave
Desert. In the middle, covering most of Nevada and Utah as well as parts
of California, Oregon, and Idaho and a smidgen of northern Arizona, is
the Great Basin, an area with no drainage to the sea. The name, given to
it by Captain John C. Frémont, is a bit of a misnomer. The Great Basin is
actually a series of about 150 alternating mountain ranges and basins, an
ecosystem that ecologists call the high desert.

The name fits perfectly. The region is high and dry, bitterly cold in
winter and hot in summer. The basins of the high desert range in altitude
from three thousand to six thousand feet, and the mountain peaks reach
twelve thousand feet. What little precipitation the Great Basin gets is
usually snow, which means almost no rain during the growing season.

The harsh climate limits the vegetation to widely spaced bunchgrass, a few forbs, and a lot of sagebrush. It is not as lush a place for wildlife as the grass-dominated Great Plains, but it suits some creatures just fine.

Small mammals, for example, abound in the Great Basin. Ground squirrels, jackrabbits, mice, and pocket gophers are common. Mule deer and pronghorns survive there because they eat shrubs as well as grasses. Bison, which rely heavily on grasses, are not present. Perhaps because large game is relatively scarce, wolves have never played much of a role in this ecosystem. The paucity of wolves (which prey on coyotes as well as pronghorns) and the abundance of small mammals make the Great Basin ideal for coyotes, where they have coexisted with pronghorns for millennia. Today, in Hart Mountain National Antelope Refuge, which lies near the northwestern edge of the Great Basin, that coexistence may be threatened.

Hart Mountain is typical high-desert terrain. Like the Great Basin, though, it has a misleading name; Hart Mountain is not really a mountain, but a jagged ridge that runs along the western edge of the refuge. To the north, it connects with Poker Jim Ridge. Together, they form a long, continuous chine that rises steeply from the floor of Warner Valley, ascending over 3,500 feet to an 8,065-foot peak. The ridge is cut by deep canyons, which carry snow melt to the valley, creating a surprising series of large lakes in this arid land. Although the lakes go dry every decade or so, Warner Valley is a haven for aquatic birds, and it is not uncommon to see gulls soaring over the desert.

The Mormons were the first permanent settlers in the Great Basin, establishing themselves in the Great Salt Lake Valley in 1847. No one knows when the first permanent settlers reached Hart Mountain, but until 1860, the only inhabitants were trappers, miners, and traders.

The region was too arid to farm, so the earliest settlers used the land to graze horses and cattle. By 1873, at least one rancher had settled in Warner Valley, and Hart Mountain, with its many springs, offered an attractive summer range. The terrible winter of 1889–90 nearly wiped out cattle ranching in the Great Basin. Many cows froze or starved to death, causing some stockmen to switch to sheep.

Sheep are better browsers than cattle and do not require hay in the winter. More important, unlike cows, they can use snow as a source of water and do not have to be watered daily. This enables them to move farther from watering holes in search of forage.

Western folklore to the contrary, a properly managed flock of sheep is no harder on a range than cattle. Unfortunately, few ranchers managed their sheep properly, and ranges that had already been overgrazed by cattle were soon overgrazed by sheep. In the Great Basin, much of the grazing land was owned by the government, so there was little incentive for conservation. Whoever got there first used the range—and often abused it. That was the situation in south-central Oregon and northern Nevada in the late 1920s, when the government became concerned about the dearth of pronghorns.

The government was behind the curve; the plight of the antelopes had already stimulated action by conservationists. After pushing through state hunting bans, those groups turned their attention to establishing a pronghorn preserve. The National Audubon Society and the Boone and Crockett Club (an organization devoted to preserving and hunting big game) took the first step. They bought part of the Last Chance Ranch in northern Nevada and gave it to the government. That land became the nucleus of the 575,000-acre Charles Sheldon Wild Life Refuge, established by Herbert Hoover on January 26, 1931. The executive order creating the refuge did not have the word *antelope* or *pronghorn* in it.

That oversight was rectified five years later by President Franklin Roosevelt, who established the 275,000-acre Hart Mountain Antelope Refuge to serve as a warm-season range for the pronghorns that wintered at Sheldon. In 1978, the two refuges were combined into a single unit, which is called the Sheldon/Hart Mountain Complex. The two do not abut one another, and despite the difference in the size of the ranges, the pronghorns spend most of their time at Hart Mountain, retreating to

Sheldon only when winter weather becomes severe.

Because of overgrazing, the range at Hart Mountain was in poor condition. To rehabilitate it, the new managers ordered the removal of sheep. The following year, the first census was taken at Hart Mountain; the count was twenty-three hundred pronghorns.

No one knows how many coyotes were present at the time, but their numbers were probably low. In *A Hole in the Sky*, a memoir about growing up on a cattle ranch in Warner Valley, William Kittredge explained the local methods of coyote control and estimated their effectiveness: "We baited the coyotes with 1080 [Compound 1080 is a deadly poison that was often used on coyotes] and hunted them from airplanes; we wiped them out."

Since there were few coyotes to contend with and sheep were off the range, pronghorns appeared to be set to multiply. But instead, the population did the opposite; it began to drop.

To find out why, I look up Victoria Roberts, the outdoor recreation planner for Hart Mountain National Antelope Refuge and the woman who serves as the refuge's spokesperson when visiting journalists come to town.

The refuge's headquarters are on the second and third floors of the Lakeview, Oregon, post office. Victoria (or, as she prefers, Tory) and I meet there in a large room whose walls are covered with charts and graphs and maps. She is in her early thirties and has long, brown hair. Her mien is serious, her gaze direct. I know from previous conversations that she is not a biologist but a history major with a degree from the University of Oregon. I also know that she is knowledgeable about the ecology of the refuge.

Before we start, she hands me a graph, a plot of the pronghorn population on the refuge from 1937 to 1998. The graph resembles a cross section of a mixing bowl with dough dribbling over the right edge.

From 1937 to 1955, the number of pronghorns on the refuge declined by 90 percent to about two hundred (the left side of the bowl). It then held steady until the mid-1970s, varying between two hundred and five hundred (the bottom of the bowl). Later in that decade, the numbers began to inch up, and in the 1980s, they rose steeply, peaking in the early 1990s at about nineteen hundred (the right side of the bowl). Since then, they have declined again (the dribble of dough). In 1998, the count was nine hundred antelopes.

The two precipitous declines in pronghorns on a refuge that was set up specifically to preserve the species are the kinds of things that give refuge managers the willies. Especially considering that the total pronghorn population has risen from its low in 1915 to about one million today. Which led to my first question to Tory Roberts: "Why haven't the refuge's pronghorns kept pace with the growth of the rest of the population?"

"First, there may be a problem with the data. Three different counting techniques were used. In the old days, they went out on horseback and on foot and estimated the number from what they counted. In the early 1950s, we began using airplanes, and in the mid-1980s, we switched to helicopter surveys."

"But the general trends? Do you believe them?"

Tory doesn't hesitate. "Yes, I do."

"Then why did the population decline between the time the refuge was formed and the 1950s? You establish a refuge to protect pronghorns, and the population immediately begins to drop?"

She smiles wryly. "Doesn't look good, does it? There was a series of severe winters back then. That may have had something to do with it. Climate has a big impact on desert ecosystems, because it's so variable. Also, sheep were removed from the refuge and replaced by cattle. I've heard all kinds of other theories, too. Sunspots, for example. And somebody tried to link it with the nuclear testing that was going on in Nevada. Who knows?"

"What about today? What's happening now?"

"We're trying to improve habitat. Cattle grazing was stopped on the refuge in 1991. We've begun to do controlled burns. Mike Dunbar, our staff biologist, has talked to researchers who have been coming here for years, and they say the range looks better than it has ever looked."

I have read the reports, and I know about the hard work that has gone into improving the range. I hate to ask the next question, but it is the crux of the matter. "Then why is the pronghorn population dropping?"

The refuge had suspected for years that coyote predation on fawns was the problem, Tory says. So Mike Nunn, the refuge manager, proposed a limited coyote-control program. The program was to last three years and was to be aimed at killing coyotes on the fawning grounds just before fawning season started. In December 1995, he revealed his proposal to the public. At first, nothing happened.

"Then a large ad appeared in the *Oregonian*," Tory says, referring to the state's biggest newspaper. "The ad was placed by Friends of Animals, an animal rights group. It said that the U.S. Fish and Wildlife Service was going to kill coyotes, including shooting pups in their dens. The ad drew thirteen hundred comments."

Many of the comments came from extremists on both sides of the issue. One group thought it was a great idea and favored killing all the coyotes. The other side called the Fish and Wildlife people "assassins" or worse and held that no coyotes should be killed for any reason—ever. But there were a number of thoughtful responses from biologists and ecologists, many of whom believed that the refuge hadn't proved its case. The data to support coyote predation as the cause of high fawn mortality wasn't adequate, they suggested. Maybe the real problem was habitat. Maybe the pronghorns were missing something in their diet that increased fawn mortality. Get more data, they said. Make your case bulletproof. The refuge took the criticisms seriously and agreed to conduct a two-year study.

"That study was completed in the fall of 1997," Tory continues.

"Mortality rates and coyote predation were confirmed. Mike Dunbar is a veterinarian, and his necropsies and examinations of live antelopes showed that the animals are healthy. In December, the refuge proposed to hold a public coyote hunt on the pronghorns' fawning grounds to reduce the number of coyotes."

"What happened?"

"We got sued. The Oregon Natural Desert Association, the Predator Defense Institute, and several other environmental groups went to court to stop the hunt. Rather than fight, we called it off."

From Lookout Point, a few miles south of the refuge visitor center, the land stretches endlessly to the east. It is near dusk, and four pronghorns are watching me watch them. A ground squirrel scampers over the rocks beneath an unreadable sign that is riddled with bullet holes, and a bushy-tailed coyote zigzags through the gray sagebrush beyond the rocks. The fawning grounds are east of here, and next spring, the coyote-pronghorn struggle will resume, one more performance in a long-running play that started millennia ago.

The animals of the early grasslands where the pronghorn evolved were much more diverse than those of today. Before the Pleistocene extinctions, horses, zebras, camels, and mammoths grazed the North American plains. They were pursued by an equally diverse group of carnivores: giant bears, lions, and cheetahs competed with wolves and coyotes for meals.

On those ancient grasslands, pronghorns evolved the traits that determined their relationship with another Pleistocene survivor—the coyote. They developed incredible eyesight to spot predators at long range across the open plains. It has been said that pronghorns can see as well as humans using eight-power binoculars. That claim may be overstated, but every pronghorn expert attests to their excellent vision.

Another way pronghorns avoided predators was by using speed. Centuries of life-or-death chases with cheetahs gave them the equipment to run fast and far. They have huge lungs and hearts. They suck in oxygen through an oversized windpipe. Heavily muscled hindquarters propel their lengthy strides, which gobble up ground. The result is a very fast creature, faster than any North American animal. In fact, over long distances, they are faster than any land animal in the world.

How fast? Because pronghorns are inclined to race with cars, perhaps to show off, numbers abound. Observers swear to 40, 50, 60, and even 70 miles an hour. Arthur Einarsen described such a race in *The Pronghorn Antelope and Its Management*. The author and two passengers were driving across a dry lake bed in Lake County, Oregon (the same county in which the antelope refuge is located), when several pronghorns, led by a "magnificent buck," began to race them. "The buck was now 20 feet away and kept abreast of the car at 50 miles per hour," Einarsen wrote. "He gradually increased his gait, and with a tremendous burst of speed flattened out so that he appeared as lean and low as a greyhound. Then he turned toward us at about a 45 degree angle and disappeared in front of the car, to reappear on our left. He had gained enough to cross our course as the speedometer registered 61 miles per hour."

How fast? Even if Einarsen's speedometer wasn't perfectly accurate, we are still taking *fast*. Centuries of selective breeding have produced horses with a top speed of only about forty-three miles per hour. In any case, pronghorns are speedy enough to outrun the fastest coyote that ever lived without raising a sweat.

Speed, however, has its disadvantages. One reason pronghorns can't jump a fence is probably because they are so fast that running around things makes more sense. (Another reason might be that pronghorns evolved on grasslands, where there's not much to jump over.) But there's a more serious disadvantage to depending on sheer speed to escape predators, and it affects the young of the species.

Ungulates employ two strategies to protect their young: following and hiding.

The young of follower species stick close to Mom. Sheep, goats, and caribou are followers, as are horses and rhinoceroses. The adults protect their young from predators by leading them into difficult terrain, as mountain goats and bighorn sheep do, and by defending them with hooves and horns.

Hiders, on the other hand, do not stay with their mothers; they conceal themselves for protection. This is a sensible adaptation for a species that uses speed to elude predators. The young are simply not up to the task of outrunning a cheetah or even a wolf. Consequently, antelope fawns, which weigh only six to eight pounds at birth, are hiders. After nursing, the fawns move away from their mother. They are nearly odorless and leave no spoor that might lead predators to them. After locating a hiding place, they lie motionless in the grass for up to four hours, until the mother returns. Then they nurse and hide again, this time in a different spot. The mother stays close enough to the fawns to protect them against predators should the need arise, but not so close as to give away their position. Because pronghorns almost always have twins, which hide separately, the mother must keep an eye on both of them.

The first five days of the fawns' lives are spent hiding. During the next fifteen, they become more active but still rely primarily on hiding. Those first twenty days of life are the coyotes' window of opportunity, and they make the most of it.

Coyotes use a variety of methods to locate fawns. The simplest is called "probing." A coyote spots a lone doe and begins hunting ground squirrels or mice near her. The doe will not return to her fawns as long as the coyote is around, but if he gets too close, she will try to drive him away. Her reaction alerts the coyote that a fawn is in the neighborhood. His search becomes more intensive. The coyote may not find a fawn, in which case it ends up with a few mice for dinner. But he might get lucky and stumble across one. If he does, the end comes mercifully quickly. A bite behind the head and a powerful shake kill the fawn.

Dr. Joy Belsky, an ecologist with the Oregon Natural Desert Association, was one of the people behind the lawsuit that stopped the coyote hunt the refuge proposed for the spring of 1998. She objected to it because she didn't believe the refuge was using the best science available and because it wasn't following its own management plan, which was published in 1994 and made habitat restoration—not predator control—its main goal. Also, she didn't think it would help the pronghorns.

"To really reduce fawn mortality," she says, "you would have to kill a lot of coyotes, far more than the refuge is proposing." But a more important reason is a philosophical difference with the refuge manager.

"There's been a paradigm shift in wildlife management," says Joy. "Mike Nunn is a throwback to the old-style wildlife manager of thirty or forty years ago. Back then, the idea was to manage intensively for a single species. Today, wildlife managers try to improve habitat, and let the chips fall where they may for a given species. Who knows what the proper balance between coyotes and pronghorns should be?"

I mention the census data that showed over two thousand pronghorns on the refuge in 1937, when the range was run-down after being overgrazed by cattle and sheep.

Joy says the data before the 1950s—before the refuge began using aircraft to conduct its censuses—look suspicious to her; she believes that the counts from the early years were far too high. She also points out that pronghorn populations were low in the 1950s even though the refuge had an intensive predator-control program, and that the antelopes' numbers increased in the 1970s after that program was discontinued.

"This is a living laboratory," she says. "An exciting experiment is going on out there. It's one of the few places in the arid West where cattle have been taken off the range. And I can't wait to see what happens. Pronghorn populations move in natural cycles. We're in a downcycle now, but they'll come back. Pronghorns and coyotes have lived together for a long time, and the pronghorns survived without human predator control."

Not everybody agrees. "The way I look at it is that this is a pronghorn refuge," Tory Roberts tells me in our last interview. "It says so in our name. Managing for pronghorns is just as important and valid as managing for California condors or Florida panthers. We manage today with a much greater ecosystem approach than we might have when the refuge was established, but we're still managing for pronghorns."

The issue is a complicated one, but it can be reduced to one difficult question: Is the main purpose of national wildlife refuges to preserve species or to maintain and restore ecosystems? Almost every ecologist believes that a healthy ecosystem is essential to good wildlife management. But if California condors were being eaten by coyotes, many of them would probably support some form of predator control, regardless of the health of the ecosystem. Of course, condors are an endangered species, while pronghorns are plentiful.

But there is evidence that limited coyote control can help pronghorns. John Byers's data from the National Bison Range, which spans fifteen years, suggests that killing coyotes just before fawning season significantly reduces pronghorn mortality. In those years when no coyotes were killed, fawn mortality averaged 91 percent. When one or more was killed, fawn mortality dropped to 84 percent. And in 1995, when hunters shot fourteen coyotes—the most killed during the study—mortality was only 56 percent.

Mike Nunn says, "I don't think, I *know* that coyote control benefits pronghorns." And he says he can cite studies that back him up.

The real question, of course, is this: What is the proper—the natural—balance between the two species at the refuge? And since it is a dynamic system, how do those populations change over time? Those are the questions Joy Belsky would like to see answered. Mike Nunn, on the other hand, believes that Hart Mountain, as large as it is, it is not a fully functional ecosystem. The refuge is ringed by ranches and Bureau of Land Management property where cattle grazing is permitted. Humans may have influenced the ecosystem in ways we don't completely understand, he says, and we may have given coyotes the upper hand. In other words, achieving a "natural" balance between coyotes and pronghorns on the refuge is not possible because humans have altered the ecosystem. Consequently, he favors active management for pronghorns.

"Coyotes are neat animals," he says. "They belong at Hart Mountain. We don't want to eliminate coyotes, just control them on the fawning grounds before fawning season."

The National Wildlife Refuge System Improvement Act of 1997 appears to be on his side. It mandates that "every refuge be managed to fulfill the Refuge System Mission [to conserve and restore wildlife and habitats] as well as the specific purpose(s) for which the refuge was established." In this case, the refuge was established for pronghorns, so the refuge wants to manage for pronghorns. And if that means whacking a few coyotes, then so be it. Mike Nunn believes that he is just doing his job, and he finds the tactics employed by animal-rights groups and the Oregon Natural Desert Association "very frustrating." He is not opposed to Joy Belsky's "exciting experiment," he just doesn't believe that conducting it should be the responsibility of the national wildlife refuge system.

Meanwhile, with no spring hunt, fawn mortalities for 1998 were high. Tory Roberts gives me the results. "We had 1,303 fawns born this year," she intones. "Eighty-three survived. That's a mortality rate of 94 percent."

"How do you know coyotes were the culprits?"

"Necropsies, blood analysis, and sight evidence. Also, we tagged twenty-seven fawns. None of them survived. One was stillborn, and one died of starvation. A bobcat got one and a golden eagle another one. Coyotes got the other twenty-three."

CHAPTER 9

The Science of Muddling Through

Bon Secour National Wildlife Refuge, Alabama

Dr. SAM PEARSALL has a rumpled, mischievous look that belies his neat desk and serious job. He is director of science of the North Carolina chapter of The Nature Conservancy and oversees the sixty-one sites the conservancy owns in the state. He also helps decide which new sites the organization will acquire, which is why I am in his office on a fine spring afternoon.

"It's not that hard," he says with a hint of a twang from his native state of Tennessee. "We apply several criteria in selecting a site. First, are there multiple populations of vulnerable species at the site? Second, is it threatened? Third, is there opportunity? Is the site for sale, or better yet, does someone want to give it to you?

"With these criteria in mind, we apply basic management principle number one, which I call 'the science of muddling through.' It came from an article published back in the 1950s. It says that the best decisions are made by people who operate on the information at hand to make decisions that seem to move them in the right direction and that foreclose as few options as possible. I'm a big believer in that. I think that logical, heuristic planning frameworks seldom work real well. I'm an incrementalist."

Sam's approach to acquiring nature preserves came to mind during my visit to Bon Secour National Wildlife Refuge several months later. The refuge is a prime example of what can happen when determined men and women with a clearly defined objective apply Sam's method. The way that group went about saving the land that became the nucleus of the Bon Secour refuge offers a lesson to anyone interested in establishing a wildlife sanctuary.

And while I was there, I saw other examples of how the science of muddling through works. One involved a bird, one of the many species of warblers that frequent the refuge, and the other came from a woman I met whose life was changed by a fortuitous incremental decision.

The Pine Beach Trail starts in a parking lot under a sprawling live oak festooned with Spanish moss. It leads southeast along an old sand road into the heart of Bon Secour, a refuge known for its abundance of birds and bird species. Red basil grows beneath a mixed forest of oaks and pines. Its bright, spikelike flowers are said to attract hummingbirds. Nearby, beautyberry shrubs are covered with purple berries. Farther along are sparkleberry and gallberry. In fact, berries are everywhere along the trail. Only one thing is missing: the birds that are supposed to feed on them, the Neotropical migrants—especially the warblers—that have made this refuge famous.

Bon Secour consists of several parcels of land scattered along a skinny east-west peninsula on the Alabama coast. To the north of the peninsula is Mobile Bay; to the south is the Gulf of Mexico; to the west is the inlet that leads into the bay. The nearest town is Gulf Shores, which bills itself as "America's Riviera." But the college students who congregate there during spring break consider that name a bit fancy and have long called it the "Redneck Riviera."

Yet the name of the refuge, which is French for "safe harbor," is entirely appropriate. Bon Secour is an important staging area for migrating birds and butterflies. In the spring, it is the first land encountered by many migrants flying north across the Gulf of Mexico. Sometimes, the migrants are exhausted after their long flights. They are often close to starvation and require food to replenish themselves. These migrants desperately need what the refuge offers—a safe harbor.

Bon Secour is an equally important stopover in the fall. Migrants pour into the refuge to stock up on food before continuing their journeys. Some of them head east toward Florida, some go west down the shoreline, and others take off on a direct flight across the Gulf. A few like the refuge so well that they winter here. But today, in late October, I have seen only blue jays and cardinals. Where, I wonder, are Bon Secour's supposedly abundant migratory birds?

Gator Lake, a grass-rimmed expanse of blue water, lies about a mile from the trailhead. A sign in a gazebo there rubs in my failure: "Bon Secour supports over 125 wintering, 100 resident, and 49 nonresident species of birds. During a peak year, well over 2 million individual birds may be present on the refuge at one time." Two million birds? Where?

After finishing the trail with a list of bird sightings shorter than a haiku, I decide to get some advice from the refuge's best-known birder.

Paul Blevins is a retired engineer who worked on oil-field supply boats in the Gulf because it was a good way to observe pelagic birds. He is a dedicated volunteer at the refuge, working here seven days a week except when he's off birding somewhere else. Because of the effort he puts in, Bon Secour allows him to live in the house that once served as the refuge office.

When I pull into his driveway, Paul is tending his garden. He is a slender, sixtyish man with closely cropped white hair. He is wearing jeans and a "Cape May Bird Observatory" T-shirt with a picture of an American redstart on it. A swarm of butterflies—mostly monarchs and Gulf fritillaries—rises from the garden when he strides briskly over to greet me.

He points out the plants in his yard, identifying them by their scientific names. "I plant them for butterflies and hummingbirds, and one or two of them for me. Had lots of black swallowtails before the weather," he says, referring to Hurricane Georges, which had slammed the Alabama coast a month earlier. "I also have twenty or thirty hummingbird feeders. They keep me pretty busy."

He says that the best birding is at Fort Morgan, which is the refuge's westernmost unit, lying at the tip of the peninsula. "The best part of the migration is over. I had over a hundred hummingbirds here in the middle of September. Most of the warblers are gone, too. All we are getting now are the stragglers. But there's a world of myrtle warblers coming back in winter plumage."

Paul tells me a couple of spots to try at Fort Morgan. He also tells me he has been volunteering at the refuge for nearly twenty years.

"You must have started young," I say.

"I'm seventy-six years old, soon will be," he says.

Seventy-six? He looks sixty, and he moves like he's fifty. Either birding is good for your health or Paul Blevins has found the Fountain of Youth at Bon Secour.

After thanking him, I drive west down the refuge road to Fort Morgan, which turns out to be an imposing array of earthworks, bunkers, and cannons. The fort was built to guard the entrance to Mobile Bay. During the Civil War, Admiral David Farragut sailed past the fort on the morning of August 5, 1864. After one of his ships hit a mine and sank, he supposedly uttered the words that brought him more fame than any of his naval victories: "Damn the torpedoes! Full speed ahead!"

The fort was pressed into service during World War I and World War II. Today, it is operated by the Alabama Historical Society, but according to Paul Blevins, it is better known for its birding than for its gun batteries. I head for one of the places near the fort that Paul recommended. Birders call it "The Stable," an area where Civil War troops kept their horses.

The Stable lies north of the road. It is heavily forested and laced with sandy paths overhung with oaks. There are lots of acorns and berries and a few catbirds but no warblers. Over thirty-five species of warblers pass through the refuge every fall, and I have yet to see even one. Of course, it might not be my fault. Most warbler species are in trouble.

Warblers are getting hit at both ends of their migration. Take, for example, the cerulean warbler, which Bon Secour lists as an uncommon species in the fall. In the last twenty-five years, its population has dropped 60 percent. These warblers winter in a part of the Andes that is being converted to coffee plantations. The North American forests in which they nest are also being lost to agriculture, and what's left of the forests they prefer is being fragmented by roads and development. The loss of deep woods has made the species increasingly vulnerable to predators and nest parasites such as raccoons and brown-headed cowbirds, which thrive in fragmented forests. Recent research has shown that in forest fragments of twenty-five acres or less, 25 to 100 percent of songbird nests are lost to predation.

The double whammy of lost wintering grounds and fragmented breeding areas has reduced songbird populations—including those of most warblers—throughout the United States. Maybe the reason I'm not seeing any warblers at Bon Secour is because there aren't many to see. Or maybe I just got here too late in the season.

The last site Paul Blevins recommended was the "Middle Ground." It lies on the south side of the peninsula, so I trudge across the road into a scraggly field dotted with groves of young slash pines. Monarchs are everywhere, loading up on nectar for their flight across the Gulf to their wintering sites in Mexico. Ducks, geese, and pelicans fly low over the water, avoiding gas rigs, those huge structures that rise from the water on steel legs—and that are all too common along this part of the Gulf Coast.

Beyond the pines lies an abandoned World War II airstrip, overgrown but still visible. Suddenly, as if by magic, a flock of forty or fifty warblers appears above it. Then the floodgates open. Flock after flock of warblers flies down the length of the old airstrip, heading west. Some of the birds drop into the pines at the edge of the field, where they flit about, occasionally flashing a yellow rump. No doubt about it, these are myrtle warblers. Paul Blevins used the old name for them, the name assigned to the eastern species before ornithologists combined it with Audubon's warbler, its western counterpart, in 1973. Today, both myrtle and Audubon's warblers are considered members of a single widespread species, the yellow-rumped warbler.

Unlike most of the other fifty-five species of North American warblers, the yellow-rump is holding its own throughout its range, which is most of the continent. And surveys indicate that the eastern population is increasing. Clearly, yellow-rumps are doing something right.

The yellow-rumped warbler, *Dendroica coronata*, is a six-inch-long, rather undistinguished-looking bird that weighs less than one ounce. Its winter markings are a streaked breast and a pronounced yellow patch on its rump. The yellow-rump's summer plumage is more colorful, thanks to the addition of distinct yellow patches on its wings (which are there in winter, too, but are less conspicuous) and another yellow spot, on its crown. Somehow, this tiny ball of feathers has adapted and flourished as we humans have changed the face of North America with roads and farms, parking lots and houses.

Like the coyote and a few other species, the yellow-rump is a generalist, which is often given as the reason for its success. It is not picky about its nest sites; all it needs is a few conifers. This allows it to breed almost anywhere in northern North America, from Alaska to Newfoundland. Contrast this with the rare Kirtland's warbler, which breeds only in certain jack-pine barrens in a few counties in Michigan. Also, yellow-rumps fledge quickly and leave the nest within two weeks of hatching, after which the parents often begin a second brood, a progenitive habit that apparently compensates for losses to predators and parasites.

The yellow-rump's diet is as catholic as its nesting requirements. Most warblers are insectivores, but the yellow-rump relishes berries and seeds as well as insects. In fact, the name of the eastern race comes from its fondness for the fruit of bayberry bushes, also known as wax myrtles. Because they don't depend entirely on insects, yellow-rumps can tolerate cold snaps that send insectivorous warblers migrating south.

Biologists define *true migration* as a process that occurs between relatively fixed sites, often by direct flight. Kirtland's warbler, for example, always summers in Michigan and winters in the Bahamas. And as we have seen, the entire eastern population of monarch butterflies, although widespread across their breeding grounds, winters only at a few sites in Mexico.

Yellow-rumped warblers, on the other hand, follow a different and more flexible plan, called a *facultative migration*. In biology, the word *facultative* is used to refer to an organism that can react in more than one way to a stimulus. A facultative annual, for example, is a plant that sometimes completes its life cycle in twelve months and sometimes doesn't, depending on conditions. Birds that undertake facultative migrations decide day to day when and if to migrate, in which direction they should move, and how far they should go. The result is a disorderly migration that varies from year to year, with an overall southerly drift in the fall and the reverse in the spring. This describes the meanderings of the yellow-rumped warbler pretty well.

Yellow-rumps winter as far north as Massachusetts and as far south as Panama. At one time or another, they have been spotted in almost all of the Caribbean islands and Central American countries and in the Farallon Islands off the coast of California. Ornithologist Arthur Cleveland Bent devoted over three pages to sightings of these warblers. Over the course of a year, they can be found almost anywhere in North America. Furthermore, they depart and arrive at different times, which makes them very unpredictable migrants. At least to us. As far as the birds are concerned, they're just doing what makes good sense.

Long migrations, especially over water, are dangerous undertakings, particularly for small birds and insects (which is probably why few insects migrate). An unexpected storm or a headwind or lack of fat reserves can exhaust them over the sea. Monarchs coming across the Gulf from Mexico in inclement weather have dropped onto passing sailboats when fatigue overtook them, turning decks and riggings orange with their bright wings.

At Bon Secour, tired birds coming in from the Gulf sometimes literally fall from the sky into the nearest tree when they reach land. So common is this phenomenon that birders have given it a name: *fallout*. Paul Blevins has seen two fallouts. "You are watching a tree," he says. "Suddenly, there's a multitude of colors on a green background. The live oaks just disappear with all those different warblers."

Because migration is a risky business, birds undertake it only because they must, either to stay warm or find food or both. Like most warblers, yellow-rumps have to migrate; they would not survive winter in the far north. But because of their flexibility in nesting sites and diet, they can avoid the dangerous long-distance, nonstop flights that many other warblers make. This less hazardous, we'll-go-when-we-feel-like-it-and-only-as-far-as-we-choose approach to migration—combined with the species' fecundity, widespread distribution, and overall flexibility—has helped yellow-rumps wax while other warbler have waned. This lack of preprogrammed behavior is the hallmark of a generalist.

The success of generalists such as coyotes and yellow-rumps leads one to wonder why all species aren't generalists. If generalists hold the winning hand, why specialize? The answer is complex. Specialized species can usually outforage generalists as long as the conditions under which they honed their skills remain unchanged. Wolves specialize in bringing down big game, and in a land full of bison, pronghorns, and deer, wolves easily outcompete coyotes. Furthermore, their larger size allows them to kill the coyotes or drive them away. But if times change and big game becomes scarce, coyotes, which can subsist on carrion and mice, will survive, while wolves will decline. During periods of change, generalists—with their adaptability, their ability to muddle through—fare better than specialists. And ever since Europeans came to North America, rapid change has been the order of the day.

These changes have reduced the continent's biodiversity. The ivory-billed woodpecker, the great auk, and other plant and animal species have become extinct in the last few centuries. Worldwide, the situation is even worse. The amount of land required to support the ever-increasing population of humans has wiped out many species that were unable to adapt. This has led some ecologists to worry that another great spasm of extinctions—like the one that did in the dinosaurs—is upon us.

In this apocalyptic view, the only wildlife left will be generalists, the so-called weedy species. In an excellent but exceedingly pessimistic essay entitled "Planet of Weeds," David Quammen said that the wildlife of the future will consist of coyotes, rats, cockroaches, and a few other generalists. He didn't mention yellow-rumped warblers, but I'd like to add them to the list. Even if his predictions are accurate—and I suspect and hope they are not—yellow-rumps would surely brighten up the dark future he envisions.

⤳

Jack Friend and his wife, Venetia, join me for dinner one night at a Gulf Shores restaurant. They are a well-scrubbed, well-dressed, attractive couple. Jack is a retired market research consultant who played an important role in establishing Bon Secour as a wildlife refuge. Venetia is an excellent birder. They agreed to meet me to tell me how the refuge came to be.

"It's hard to believe, even today," he says over the murmur of the crowd. "Richard Gaynor and his family owned a cottage in what is now the middle of the refuge. Richard and I were friends. His dad had built this little house, this cottage down on the beach, before World War II. On Friday afternoon, he would pack his family—and sometimes me—in the big LaSalle that he drove. We would arrive as the sun was going down. His father would gig flounder till about 2 A.M. Then he would come in and hit the sack. Except for one neighbor, there was nobody else down there. It was wild, the most beautiful place. Richard had a big old red dog, and after supper, the three of us would go hunting for wild pigs. When we got older, we would come over by ourselves and hunt ducks on the lagoon. I really developed a love for that place."

"Back then," Venetia adds, "there were no gas rigs in the Gulf, no lights on the beach. Plenty of turtles."

"We took it for granted," Jack says. "You loved it, but you took it for granted. In any case, I bought a house down there myself. Later, I learned that a real-estate developer was getting ready to buy up what we called the Perdue property—about twelve hundred acres that looped around the lagoon. The plan was to build 5,747 housing units, a hotel, a commercial center. Some of us—people who had been going down there for years—got together and formed a committee to stop it."

From a stack of file folders on the chair next to him, Jack pulls out letter after letter—to the governor, to his congressman, to the United States Fish and Wildlife Service, to The Nature Conservancy. He stresses that he was not the only person involved and rattles off the names of the men and women who participated. "In the beginning," he says, "we had no plan, except to write letters and make phone calls, each person pushing his or her particular interest."

If birds would sway someone, they talked about birds. If another person was interested in sea turtles, they mentioned sea turtles. One enterprising committee member discovered a rare mouse on the property, and the Alabama beach mouse, which was later listed as an endangered species, was used to influence other people. The approach resembled the facultative migration of the yellow-rumped warbler—go here if the situation warrants it, go there if conditions change. It was a perfect example of Sam Pearsall's muddling-through approach, intelligently applied.

And like the yellow-rumps, the group succeeded. The flurry of let-ters, the hundreds of phone calls got The Nature Conservancy interested, and it bought the Perdue tract in 1979. Two years later, Fish and Wildlife acquired the land from the conservancy and established Bon Secour Na-tional Wildlife Refuge. Since then, the refuge has grown to sixty-four hundred acres and built a new headquarters. But one thing has remained unchanged; the old headquarters is still occupied by a lover of this pen-insula, Paul Blevins.

At Bon Secour's Fort Morgan unit, a sandy track leads south from the main peninsula road to the beach. It is nearing the end of a warm, sun-shine-filled day. A salty breeze blows off the Gulf. I saw in the neighbor-hood of five hundred warblers in the fields and woods west of here, mostly yellow-rumps and a few pine and palm warblers. But here on the beach, the only birds in sight are pelicans.

Several flocks of ten or more birds circle and dive; they smash into the water, bob to the surface, swallow their catch, and then flap labori-ously into the air again. In the crepuscular light, ghost crabs begin to emerge from their holes. Come nightfall, this shore will belong to them. And next summer, after the loggerheads have come to lay their eggs, these crabs will form a deadly gauntlet for the hatchlings to run before they reach the relative safety of the surf.

Bon Secour's undeveloped beaches provide a safe harbor for nesting sea turtles, but its strategic location as a staging area for migrating birds and butterflies is its most important function. However, neither birds nor turtles motivated Jack Friend and his committee. They were not a save-the-animals group; most of them simply wanted to preserve a natural area where they had spent many enjoyable days as youths.

This is not uncommon; wildlife sanctuaries are often created for rea-sons that are unrelated to the purposes they end up serving. As we have seen, Mattamuskeet National Wildlife Refuge was established to protect Canada geese, but few Canadas frequent it today. And Hart Mountain, our only national antelope refuge, is no longer critical to the survival of its eponym; indeed, if the coyotes are not controlled, antelopes may disappear entirely from that refuge.

Although most sanctuaries, such as Mexico's monarch butterfly preserve, do benefit the species they were established to protect, some of them wind up aiding other wildlife. Mattamuskeet has become a premier refuge for tundra swans, and Hart Mountain provides a home for California bighorn sheep, mule deer, and other species. Only 6.3 percent of the planet consists of protected natural areas, and anytime we can add to that total, we are doing wildlife a favor. In the movie *Field of Dreams*, the mantra was "Build it and they will come." In wildlife management, an appropriate saying might be "Preserve it and they will come."

Katrina Davis, the office manager at Bon Secour, has long, brown hair, a big smile, and a story to tell. She and her ex-husband are from the Birmingham area; they moved to Alaska in the 1970s because, as she puts it, "the old families and corporations owned everything" in Alabama.

They started life there in a 1952 school bus on the outskirts of Fairbanks, then built a one-room cabin. "From 1979 to 1986, we lived without plumbing and electricity. I did the whole sourdough route. It was tough chopping firewood at fifty or sixty below zero. I wanted electricity, so I got a job with Fish and Wildlife in 1984, working for the Yukon Flats refuge. In 1986, we got electricity."

But like another Southerner, Robert W. Service's fictional Sam McGee, who got so cold in Alaska that he enjoyed being cremated because of the warmth, Katrina longed for a warmer climate. So when she was offered a transfer back to Alabama, to Bon Secour, she grabbed it.

She likes the area, but her time here has made her pessimistic about the future. Condos are sprouting along the beaches like, well, weeds, and

Gulf Shores is growing rapidly. "So many people are moving to the coast that it's changing the face of the beach," she says. "The big condominiums bulldoze down the sand dunes, and they're destroying the coastline. The beach at the pavilion at Gulf Shores used to be a quarter of a mile wide, not ten feet. During spring break, there was an ad in the paper that said, 'Where are the beaches?' Water was crashing into the stairs.

"Neotropicals are starving to death because we are bulldozing down their food sources. And illegal or not, developers are covering the wetlands. The loophole is that if you build on pilings, you're not going to disturb the wetlands. Now, don't you know that a duck's going to be flying over, 'Yeah, honey, our old nesting site's still there, even though there's a house on top. Let's go down there and build our nest.' It doesn't happen. Education! That's what we need more of. It's scary to think about what's going on out there. Pollution and ozone. I'll be glad to be dead in fifty years."

Given her big smile and bubbling laugh, it's hard to believe that she really means it. But she does. She believes the world has its priorities wrong and is heading for environmental disaster. Fortunately, she has found her own island of hope. And in a country where government is sometimes despised and almost always considered irrelevant, Katrina Davis—whose only plan was to bring electricity to her cabin—wound up working for a government agency that she adores.

"I could make more if I went and worked for a lawyer," she tells me. "But I'd feel like I'd be nothing more than a paper pusher. I feel like, even though I'm a small cog in a big machine, the machine is working for a greater purpose. I feel like my life has a purpose, working for Fish and Wildlife Service. I feel part not only of a family but of an organization that takes pride in the environment and animals. I'm just real proud to work here."

It's nice to feel that good about one's employer. And Katrina arrived in her felicitous situation in the same unplanned way that Jack Friend and the other members of the committee proceeded to save Bon Secour from development, in the same way that Sam Pearsall manages his work for The Nature Conservancy, and in the same facultative way that the yellow-rumped warbler migrates, just making one reasonable decision after another.

The specialists' set patterns of behavior have a place in the world, but the generalists' method of just muddling through seems to work well, too. And if we use it as well as Sam Pearsall and Jack Friend have in acquiring natural areas and protecting them from the bulldozers, then we can make more room for the specialists and avoid becoming a planet of weeds.

$\mathcal{W}$here the Wild Goose Goes

Horicon National Wildlife Refuge, Wisconsin

IF YOU DRIVE across Horicon National Wildlife Refuge on Highway 49 on a fall afternoon, you will see skein after skein of Canada geese streaming into the marsh, a wild tangle of cattails glowing golden brown in the slanting rays of the sun. So abundant are the geese and so primeval looking is the marsh that you could almost believe—if the pavement and your car weren't there—that you have been transported back in time, that you are seeing what this land looked like before it was settled. But you would be wrong. Before men began monkeying around with Horicon Marsh, neither cattails nor geese were present in anything like their current abundance. And how they came to be here is a story that began ten thousand years ago when the Green Bay Lobe of the Wisconsin glacier retreated north.

The receding glacier left a thirty-thousand-acre oval-shaped gouge along the Rock River in south-central Wisconsin. The moraine deposited by the glacier obstructed the south-flowing river, forming a lake. When the moraine eroded away, water levels dropped and left a rich, silt-filled basin that was periodically flooded by the river. In those flood plains, a marsh developed.

The Northern pike, ducks, deer, wild rice, and cranberries of the marsh attracted Indians. Numerous tribes hunted and fished and gathered wild plants there, and the Winnebagos built towns around it. The southernmost of these was Elk Village, which consisted of six lodges and 110 people.

When white settlers arrived in the area, farmers spread out along the edges of the marsh. Soon, most of the Winnebagos were gone, victims of a dreary con game that persuaded them to cede their lands to the government and move west. In 1846, the settlers founded a town where Elk Village had stood. They called it Horicon at the insistence of one settler who hailed from Lake George, New York, and who believed that Horicon was the original name of his hometown lake. The marsh became Winnebago Marsh, and the settlers immediately set about altering it. Over the years, the name of the marsh has changed, but the tradition of manipulating it has persisted.

The first step was to erect a dam. The water power was used to run a sawmill and a gristmill. The dam also inadvertently re-created the ancient lake that had formed the marsh. The new lake was fourteen miles long and six miles across. The settlers named it Lake Horicon and claimed it was the largest man-made lake in the world. Boats plied the lake, and rafts of logs were floated down it to the sawmill in Horicon.

But the new lake had flooded many of the farms along the edge of the marsh. The farmers sued the dam builders, who eventually gave in. In 1869, the dam was breached, and Horicon Lake became Horicon Marsh. Three years later, the state of Wisconsin sold almost twenty thousand acres of the marsh to a state senator, Saterlee Clark, and some partners for nine cents an acre.

The resurrected marsh was almost as productive as the original. The owners leased it to gun clubs, whose wealthy members came up from the cities for the outstanding duck hunting. One resident estimated that half a million ducks used the marsh. Countless muskrats built their lodges in the marsh and lived their secretive lives there.

Unfortunately, the next attempt to manipulate the marsh was to have a far greater and longer-lasting impact on the ecosystem than the temporary damming of the Rock River.

In 1904, a group of developers bought eighteen thousand acres of Horicon Marsh. Its plan was to drain the marsh and convert it to farmland. The scheme was opposed by hunters, who feared the loss of waterfowl shooting, and supported by farmers, who foresaw the end of the spring floods that swamped their marsh-side farms. But draining wetlands was a popular pastime in the early twentieth century (as we have seen in the story of the drainage project at what is now Mattamuskeet National Wildlife Refuge), so the farmers won.

A long, straight ditch (still there today and known as the Main Ditch) was dredged down the center of the marsh in a north-south direction; it paralleled the Rock River and straightened and deepened the channel. Lateral ditches were dug to help drain the marsh. And as easy as that, a marsh that had been millennia in the making was destroyed. The moist-soil plants—the wild rice and cranberries and smartweed that had flourished in the flood plains of the Rock River—withered and died. The ducks no longer stopped there, and muskrats and deer became scarce.

But worst of all were the fires. The passing centuries had turned the silt from the ancient glacial lake and the marsh's decaying vegetation into peat, which was now dry and flammable. A dropped match or cigarette could ignite the marsh, starting slow-burning, smoky peat fires that could smolder for weeks. One firsthand account described such a fire (Gard 1972): "In 1910, it was so light all through this country around the Marsh that you could read the paper at midnight. And the whole thing was a spectacle . . . great shoots of fire coming up and a glow over the whole thing, and where the peat was burning you could see a kind of low glow coming from the earth, and the water, what there was would glow, too.

And you could hear the fire cracking, and you sat there and thought of the poor animals caught in it."

The fight to prevent or correct an environmental disaster is often led by one person. John Muir saved Yosemite Valley; President Theodore Roosevelt, without consultation or committees, established our system of wildlife refuges to protect birds; and Rachel Carson almost single-handedly got DDT banned in the United States. Horicon was fortunate to have such a person, one who would fight to reclaim the marsh. His name was Louis "Curley" Radke.

His idea was to reflood the marsh by building a new dam at the town of Horicon, on the same site as the ancient glacial dam and the short-lived dam of 1846. Radke, assisted by the Izaak Walton League, got 115,000 citizens to sign petitions asking the state to construct a new dam. In 1927, the Wisconsin legislature passed the Horicon Marsh Wildlife Refuge bill, which provided for a new dam and authorized the purchase of property in the marsh to establish a game preserve.

By the early 1940s, the state had built the dam and was backing up water into the parched marsh. It was also acquiring land in the southern third of the marsh, and the federal government was buying up the northern two-thirds. But as we have seen in earlier chapters, restoring nature is not a simple task. More manipulation of the marsh was to come. And the philosophy behind that manipulation came from a man who lived right down the road in Madison, Wisconsin, and who was restoring nature himself on some farmed-out land not far from Horicon Marsh.

In April 1935, Aldo Leopold, then forty-eight years of age, bought a small farm near Baraboo, Wisconsin, about fifty miles west of Horicon Marsh. It was a beat-up place graced only by a line of lonely elms and a chicken coop. Over the years, Leopold and his family planted pines and transformed the chicken coop into a livable structure that they called "the Shack."

Two years earlier, Charles Scribner's Sons had published Leopold's first book, *Game Management*. Although the book is not as famous as Leopold's second book, *A Sand County Almanac*, which was published sixteen years later, it spelled out many of the management practices that are used in wildlife sanctuaries throughout the world.

The ideas put forth in *Game Management* were distilled from Leopold's years at Yale and with the Forest Service. In both institutions, he followed in the footsteps of Gifford Pinchot, a Yale graduate and the first director of the Forest Service. Pinchot believed in using (not preserving) forests as renewable resources and in the concept of sustainable yield, which in those days was enough to put him in the forefront of the nascent conservation movement.

Although Leopold's ideas about preserving wilderness, so beautifully expressed in *A Sand County Almanac*, broke with this wise-use approach, *Game Management* essentially applied Pinchot's ideas to wildlife. "Both scientists and sportsmen," Leopold wrote, "see now that effective conservation requires, in addition to public sentiment and laws [protecting wildlife], a deliberate and purposeful manipulation of the environment—the same kind of manipulation that is employed in forestry."

Leopold anticipated that this concept would repel some people, so he explained the reasoning behind his position: "There are still those who shy at this prospect of a man-made game crop as something artificial and therefore repugnant. This attitude shows good taste but poor insight. Every head of wild life in this country is already artificialized, in that its existence is conditioned by economic forces. Game management merely proposes that their impact shall not remain wholly fortuitous." In other words, we humans are already modifying the environment, so why not modify it in a way that helps wildlife?

Managing for wildlife conflicts with the idea of wilderness, which is usually thought of as a place where nature does the managing. This conflict is as alive today as it was when Leopold wrote his words, as we have seen at Hart Mountain National Antelope Refuge. Leopold himself was an advocate of wilderness, as well as an advocate for wildlife management. And although he never said so explicitly, it seems clear that he believed the two concepts were not mutually exclusive. Some land should remain untouched as wilderness areas; other land should be managed to benefit wildlife.

In the United States today, public lands are managed in ways that reflect both ideas. In 1964, President Lyndon Johnson signed the Wilderness Act, which authorized Congress to designate wilderness areas, places where "the earth and its community of life are untrammeled by man, where man himself is a visitor who does not remain." The legislation was supported by many environmental groups, but the one that led the fight for its passage was the Wilderness Society, an organization that Aldo Leopold had helped found and passionately championed.

Much earlier, though, in 1903, President Theodore Roosevelt, a confirmed wise-use disciple of Pinchot, had established the first national wildlife refuge, beginning a system that has now grown to over five hundred refuges, most actively managed for wildlife as Leopold advocated in *Game Management*. And one of the more intensively managed of those refuges is Horicon National Wildlife Refuge.

The new dam built at the town of Horicon proved unsatisfactory for re-creating the marsh. If water levels were raised high enough to flood the northern part of the marsh (the part managed by the federal government), it turned the southern part (the part managed by the state) into a lake. To remedy that problem, the national wildlife refuge's managers built a dike in 1951 that extended from east to west across the marsh just north of the boundary between the federal and state properties. This blocked the Main Ditch and backed up water into the northern part of the marsh. A gate in the dike could be opened or closed to raise or lower water levels in the refuge.

As water levels rose, cattails—which do well on disturbed soil in shallow, standing water—colonized the refuge, replacing the cranberries and wild rice and smartweed of the original, periodically flooded marsh. Musk-rats, which eat the roots of cattails and build their lodges out of its leaves and stalks, returned to the marsh, but ducks, which feed on moist-soil plants, came back more slowly.

To encourage them, the refuge began controlled burning of the marsh. This helped moist-soil plants get a foothold, and the ducks began to re-turn. Between 1944 and 1954, their numbers shot up from twenty-two thousand to well over a hundred thousand. The marsh was on its way to recovery. And as it recovered, somebody came up with the bright idea that Canada geese, which had never stopped at Horicon Marsh in sig-nificant numbers in the fall, would be a welcome addition at a wildlife refuge that was intended for waterfowl.

The Canada goose (*Branta canadensis*) comes in a confusing array of subspecies divided into a confusing array of populations that migrate along a confusing number of routes. But almost every goose that honked its way across the night sky above the newly established Horicon refuges belonged to a single race and a single population: *B. canadensis interior* of the Mississippi Valley population.

That population historically wintered along the Mississippi Valley from Missouri to Louisiana. During the early years of the twentieth cen-tury, hunting reduced it to a fraction of the number seen a century ear-lier. The first step toward restoring the population came in 1927, when Illinois established Horseshoe Lake Refuge in the southern tip of the state. Five years later, thirty thousand geese (most of the Mississippi Valley population) were wintering there, which angered southern hunters, who no longer had geese to shoot. But as bad as the hunting was in the South, it was about to get worse; Illinois, it turned out, wasn't the only state that could shortstop geese.

Horicon's managers employed three techniques to entice geese into the refuges. First, using the newly built dam and the newly constructed Main Dike, they raised water levels, which provided the geese with open water for resting. Second, they planted food for them, mostly corn that was sharecropped on the refuge by local farmers. Finally, they called them down with live decoys.

Bill Wheeler, a wildlife biologist and goose expert at the Wisconsin Department of Natural Resources, says that both the state and federal refuges kept captive flocks. These "call flocks" lured migrating geese into Horicon Marsh. Calling geese with live birds (as opposed to mechanical calls) is a very effective tactic; market hunters used call flocks, and when live decoys were finally banned, market hunting vanished.

The combination of open water, plentiful food, and friendly geese proved irresistible. Canadas began stopping at Horicon. On the federal refuge alone, the peak population grew from fewer than 1,000 in 1942 to 15,000 in 1952. By 1962, it was up to 105,000 geese, and by 1972, that number doubled. Not bad for a place that geese once found so unattractive that a hunter who killed one got his picture in the paper.

In fact, Horicon was awash in geese. About two-thirds of the entire Mississippi Valley population could be found resting in the marsh or feeding in the surrounding farm fields on peak fall days. Although those geese did not winter at Horicon, they began staying longer and longer. And though the number of geese in the Mississippi Valley population was much higher than it had been in the 1930s, almost no birds went farther south than Illinois.

Southern hunters complained about the huge number of geese at Horicon Marsh; local farmers complained about crop depredations; and biologists worried about the possibility of disease hitting the refuge and wiping out most of the Mississippi Valley population. Something, the reasoning went at the time, had to be done to disperse the Canada geese from Horicon Marsh. And with that inexorable bureaucratic logic, the federal government began the Goose Wars.

The objective was simple: reduce the peak fall population by half, from two hundred thousand birds to one hundred thousand. The strategy was equally simple: decrease the food planted on the refuge; harass the geese with helicopters, airplanes, airboats, and exploders (bazooka-like devices that make a loud noise that is supposed to spook geese); and reduce the open water in the marsh by lowering water levels. The government also began to develop other wetlands in the area.

The war commenced in the fall of 1976. Airplanes and airboats hazed the geese around the clock. Lower water levels exposed great mud flats that had once been open water. The geese responded by dispersing. Three years later, the peak population at Horicon National Wildlife Refuge had been more than halved to sixty-nine thousand birds. The bureaucrats, it seemed, had won the war.

The Redhead Hiking Trail begins just off Highway 49 in the far northwestern corner of the refuge. When I arrive there, the morning sky is gray and overcast, the temperature nippy, a harbinger of the bone-chilling cold that will follow when November ebbs and serious winter begins at Horicon Marsh. Geese are everywhere, forming wavering Vs in the sky and resting on ponds. So incessant is their gabbling that it eventually goes unnoticed, like Muzak on an elevator. Mallards and three swans mix with the geese on a pond near the trailhead.

The trail proceeds through brown, waist-high grasses spotted with cattail-ringed ponds. As I follow it south, deeper into the refuge, I see more and more ducks on the ponds. Unlike Canada geese, which are grazers and gleaners, ducks rarely feed in farm fields, preferring the natural vegetation in and around the ponds. But the sky is filled with geese, which are coming and going, moving from fields to ponds and vice versa.

The Goose Wars ended in the late 1970s with goose populations well down from their highs. Based on what I've seen, though, their numbers have rebounded smartly. How many geese are out here today? I have no idea, so when I finish the trail, I go to see someone who knows.

Patti Meyers, the manager of Horicon National Wildlife Refuge, has brown, curly hair, an engaging smile, and a no-nonsense way of speaking that labels her a Midwesterner as surely as if she had *Indiana* or *Illinois* tattooed on her forehead. She has a master's degree in field biology from Purdue and has spent twenty years with the Fish and Wildlife Service, all of it at midwestern refuges. Her office is cluttered with papers and books. A silhouette of two ducks is attached to a wall next to a window that looks out over the marsh.

"This past year, we had half a million Canada geese in the southern Wisconsin area," she says. "It was a mild winter, and some of them wintered here. They stayed on top of the ice for weeks. You'll see them out there with one foot tucked under a wing."

After the Goose Wars, the refuge declared a truce. But though it did nothing to entice the geese back, they came anyway. "We don't plant any food for them, but they still come," she says. "There are traffic jams on Highway 49. People park up there and sit in lawn chairs to watch the geese come into the marsh. But what we would like to do is attract more ducks. One of the problems is cattails. On other refuges where I worked, you had a few cattails, and you went out and pulled them. When I got here, we had twenty thousand acres of cattails."

Ducks don't eat cattails, which usually outcompete the moist-soil plants that they favor. Canada geese don't eat cattails either, but they don't depend on the marsh for food, feeding instead in nearby farm fields. Consequently, a cattail marsh—as long as it has ample open water—tends to attract more geese than ducks.

The other problem holding down the duck population is carp. Carp root around on the marshy bottom, uprooting the plants ducks like to eat and muddying the water. The high turbidity prevents sunlight from getting through to the remaining submergent vegetation, which eventually dies. Diane Penttila, the refuge biologist, says that trying to grow aquatic vegetation with carp in the water "is like trying to grow a lawn with pigs in it." At the refuge today, the Goose Wars may be over, but the Cattail and Carp War is under way.

Cattails are native to North America, but they have many of the characteristics of invasive exotics. They form monocultures that spread rapidly, and they are tough—some say impossible—to eliminate once they get established.

Patti Meyers has learned how to discourage cattails. "You have to prevent oxygen from getting to the roots," she says. "And it turns out that they have a way of getting oxygen down there through the dead shoots, so you have to get rid of those."

She employs several methods to eliminate the old shoots. Staff members mow them in winter when they stick out above the ice; they burn them; and they disk them. Then they flood the area with two or three feet of water. "That won't kill cattails," she says, "but it will stress them."

To accomplish the necessary flooding, the refuge is divided into seventeen units, and an elaborate system of dikes and ditches and pumps enables Patti to move water from one unit to another. A flooding over here to reduce cattails, a drawdown over there to encourage moist-soil plants. She has also eliminated muskrat trapping in some units because "rats" (as the trappers call them) help hold down the cattails.

"At Potato Lake, we burned it, we disked it, we did everything we could to that unit to encourage moist-soil vegetation. And we did it two years in a row. That third year, though, we didn't see any cattails, absolutely none, and you had the best unit. Smartweed and sedges, wonderful plants. Then we flooded it, and I went there one day, and I'll bet there were eighty thousand ducks in the lake.

"Well, the next year, it was about 50 percent cattails, and the year after that, it was 80 percent. This year, it looks like almost solid cattails. It reverted back so quickly," she says wistfully. "And we don't have the money to continue that kind of intensive management."

Today, the war between refuge and cattails resembles the trench warfare of World War I. One side advances slightly, then the other side counterattacks to regain the lost ground. But no gains or losses are ever decisive enough to declare victory or defeat.

Patti's objective is to have about 50 percent of the marsh in open water. She's close to reaching that goal, but the price has been, and will continue to be, eternal vigilance and intensive management. And though she no longer plants food for geese, they benefit from her hard work, since keeping cattails in check creates more of the open water that geese require.

The other half of Patti Meyers's problem in maintaining the marsh habitat is an exotic. Carp were introduced into this country from Germany in 1877. Originally hailed as a wonder fish, they were spread across the country by well-meaning folks before the problems they caused waterfowl were apparent. And like cattails, they are tough customers to control.

In winter, fish move into deeper water to avoid ice and to find higher oxygen levels. The state installed carp traps in the marsh's main channels in 1943. The traps worked beautifully; up to a million pounds of carp were removed from the marsh in a single year. But the trapping didn't dent the carp population, so in 1978, the feds took more drastic action.

"We did a big carp kill," Patti says. The refuge used the poison rotenone. "The carp came right back in bigger numbers. But we're going to try it again next winter. This time, right after the fish kill, we have a hatchery that's going to bring us millions of Northern pike to eat the young the surviving carp produce."

Northern pike were once the most important fish in Horicon Marsh and the Rock River. "One reason pike fare poorly today is because it's so shallow," Patti says with a sigh. "We freeze totally up. It kills the pike, but the carp survive. We've done borings in the ice, and the oxygen will be very low, less than one part per million, and the carp are fine down there in the mud. We hope to put in an aeration system to keep some areas in open water so the pike will survive. Some of them make it through winter in the Rock River, so we're not going to rotenone there."

The main reason carp dominate the marsh fishery is the usual one: human interference in the natural workings of the ecosystem. "The biggest threats to the refuge come from outside sources," Patti says. Some of the farms surrounding the refuge contribute to water pollution in the marsh, but an even bigger problem looms; the ancient basin in which the marsh sits is filling up with soil. Silting is a natural process that all marshes undergo, but farming accelerates it. A hard rain washes far more soil from a plowed field than it does from a natural prairie, and most of it ends up in the marsh. Thus, the waters of Horicon Marsh grow shallower each year, which causes the pike to decline and allows the carp to thrive.

To even wind up with a draw in the Cattail and Carp War, the refuge needs a lot of equipment: machines to dig ditches and build dikes; pumps to move water from one unit to the next; airboats to monitor the units; and aerators to keep pike alive. The equipment enables the refuge manager to engage in the "purposeful and deliberate manipulation of the environment" to benefit wildlife that Aldo Leopold advocated in *Game Management*.

And as he foresaw, this intensive management offends some wilderness purists who don't think the Fish and Wildlife Service should manage nature. When I ask how she responds to such criticisms, Patti says, "If you had an undisturbed island, I'd agree with them. But when you have a place like this that's been so ravaged, management's all you can do. If we left it alone, it would be a desert out there, with cattails and carp and that's about it."

I am genuinely astonished when I arrive in Baraboo and find no signs directing traffic to Aldo Leopold's Shack. In fact, none of the attendants at the service stations where I stop to get directions knows anything about Leopold. I had thought that the farm of the world-famous author and environmentalist would be a national shrine, or at least a local one. But here in the sand counties of Wisconsin, where Leopold worked out many of the ideas that guide the environmental movement, nobody has ever heard of him.

Finally, I try a bookstore in the center of town. The woman who runs it knows about Aldo Leopold and is gracious enough to make a few phone calls to find out where the Shack is located.

I arrive there twenty minutes later. A skinny asphalt driveway bordered by golden prairie grasses leads from the main road to the Shack. Aldo's daughter, Nina Leopold Bradley, lives in a modern ranch-style home on the property. A car is parked in front of it, and a friendly Labrador retriever greets me as I walk up the driveway. The Shack, a tiny, pitched-roofed building that is almost obscured by the tall grasses, sits fifty or so feet from the house. I've read so much by and about Leopold that I thought I would feel right at home here, on the old farm he wrote about so eloquently. Instead, I feel like an intruder.

I walk back to my car and pull out the tattered paperback edition of *A Sand County Almanac* that I often take with me when I travel. What would Leopold think of the intensive management practiced at Horicon? Not the young Leopold, not the hunter and wildlife manager who wrote *Game Management*, but the older man, the philosopher who articulated the land ethic.

"All ethics so far evolved," he wrote, "rest on a single premise: that the individual is a member of a community of interdependent parts. . . . The land ethic simply enlarges the boundaries of the community to include soils, waters, plants, and animals."

These are exactly the things that Patti Meyers worries about every day. Not about how to make money off them, but about how to reclaim and preserve them on the 21,408 acres entrusted to her. Surely, Leopold would have approved of the goings-on at Horicon Marsh. After all, his old farm and the Shack itself were labor-intensive reclamation projects. And I suspect he would have approved of calling down the geese to introduce them to the newly established refuge, for Aldo Leopold loved Canada geese as much as he loved restoring worn-out land. "On our farm," he wrote, "we measure the amplitude of our spring by two yardsticks: the number of pines planted and the number of geese that stop." And though the refuge doesn't plant pines, it is a raging success by the second measure.

I also suspect that Leopold would have enjoyed the spectacle of hundreds of cars lining the shoulder of Highway 49 while their occupants sit on lawn chairs beside them, watching geese fly into Horicon Marsh. He believed that people should be educated about the need to preserve wildlife and wilderness. And despite the intensive management required to maintain the refuge, it's hard to imagine anyone who wouldn't want to preserve the marsh and its inhabitants after listening to goose music while sitting beside Highway 49.

CHAPTER 11

Putting It All Together

NORTH AMERICAN WILDLIFE sanctuaries protect a variety of eco-systems, from the marshes at Horicon to the coral reefs of Bonaire, from the prairies at Tallgrass to the rocky Canadian islands in the Gulf of Maine. The managers of those sanctuaries manipulate the ecosystems in eco-logically sound ways to benefit wildlife. Instead of suppressing fires, as managers once did, they start them. Instead of draining and chan-neling wetlands, they preserve and restore them. Instead of importing exotics, they uproot them. Predator control, if it exists at all, is minimal.

The managers of most North American sanctuaries vigorously en-force environmental laws to protect the land and animals entrusted to them. They prohibit or severely restrict hunting and fishing; they fight development on their borders; and they control the number of visitors and limit their activities.

Because of their efforts, wildlife abounds within these protected lands and waters. Bison and butterflies, parrotfish and tundra swans, warblers and antelopes are flourishing. But as spectacular as the sanctuaries are, they harbor only a tiny fraction of earth's diversity. Other species flourish beneath the earth's crust, in its deepest oceans, and on other continents. Collectively, they form a great web of life that is astonishingly rich in biological diversity.

As many scientists have pointed out, however, this diversity is under attack, and the casualties are discouraging. But a careful examination of what's been achieved in North American sanctuaries gives reason to be hopeful, and the lessons learned here may be useful to other managers in other lands.

About 1.7 million known and a great many more yet-to-be-identified species live on earth. Estimates of the total number, both known and unknown, range from 4 million to 30 million. Although biologists are unsure of the exact number of species, they are quite sure that it is declining.

The respected Harvard biologist E. O. Wilson was one of the first scientists to sound the alarm about our planet's high rate of extinctions. He estimated that we are snuffing out twenty-seven thousand species a year. That is about a thousand to ten thousand times the normal rate, as determined from the fossil record. Professor Wilson (like almost every other biologist) attributes this abnormally high rate of extinctions to loss of habitat as land is cleared for agriculture and development.

These statistics have led some scientists to predict an impending ecological disaster in which an ever-growing population of *Homo sapiens*, whose numbers already top 5.7 billion, further degrade and fragment the world's ecosystems. When these deteriorating natural systems can no longer support the organisms that rely on them, the earth will suffer a great spasm of extinctions comparable in magnitude to the five the planet has already experienced (the most recent being the extinction of 65 million years ago that wiped out the dinosaurs). That would be an alarming decline in biological diversity, but it is even more alarming that many people respond, "So what? How does that affect me?"

Ecologists answer those questions in several ways.

The first answer is utilitarian in nature. The cure for cancer or the common cold or migraine headaches could come from a rare plant in a rain forest that is now being razed. Indeed, many medicines do come from wild plants and animals. One example is the two alkaloids discovered in the rosy periwinkle, a small plant found in Madagascar. Both chemicals proved to be potent anticancer agents that are now used to treat Hodgkin's disease and acute lymphocytic leukemia, which was nearly always fatal until the periwinkle came along.

Another answer is based on aesthetics. Wilson posited that humans have an innate love of the living organisms with which we evolved, and that to destroy them would make our lives grim, barren, and less joyful. To me, this theory, called biophilia, is undeniably true, and the numbers bear it out. In the United States alone, 110 million people engaged in some form of wildlife-related recreation in 1991, according to the Fish and Wildlife Service. Natural areas calm us as well as attract us. I have seen a group of rowdy youngsters enter a grove of redwoods with boom boxes blasting. Moments later, the music was off and the kids were speaking in reverent whispers.

Niles Eldredge of the American Museum of Natural History, the originator (with Stephen Jay Gould) of the punctuated-equilibrium theory of evolution, offered a more frightening reason for preserving natural systems. How would a sixth round of mass extinctions affect us? Well, Eldredge said, we just might go down with the ship ourselves. Without the ecosystems that provide us with oxygen, food, and other raw materials, we, too, might perish.

Only a few scientists subscribe to this doomsday scenario, but many of them see a future similar to the one David Quammen outlined in his essay "Planet of Weeds." Quammen said that humans and some wildlife would survive a sixth mass extinction, but that our lives would be impoverished. Many of today's plants and animals would be gone, and only a few "weedy" species that readily adapt to human-dominated landscapes would thrive. Coyotes might still cruise Hart Mountain, and carp might still swim among the cattails at Horicon Marsh, but pronghorns and Northern pike would be missing.

The future envisioned by the managers of the North American wildlife sanctuaries I visited was quite different. Most of them were reasonably optimistic. And the wildlife they managed was abundant, often more abundant than it was at the beginning of the twentieth century. Populations of pronghorns, bison, wood storks, and many other species have rebounded from their lows, and some species such as Canada geese may be at all-time highs. In many ways, we seem to be making environmental progress, rather than losing ground.

Which leads to a question: How could what I saw during my travels differ so much from the gloomy outlook expressed by scientists and other writers?

First, I confined my visits to wildlife sanctuaries, where ecosystems were being maintained or restored, so I never encountered the habitat destruction that many ecologists find so worrisome. And because the sanctuary managers I interviewed were preserving or augmenting habitat, few of them were concerned about losing species. Had I visited privately owned or poorly managed lands, I would have seen a considerably drearier picture.

Second, I traveled only in North America. Most of the countries on this continent are working hard to preserve biodiversity. An entirely different perspective would have emerged had I visited parts of the Amazon basin or Madagascar or Malaysia, where forests are being cleared and species are being lost at heartbreaking rates.

That doesn't mean that North America is problem free. The large-scale logging in Central American countries like Honduras and in some United States national forests is enough to drive the mildest-mannered conservationist to despair. And virtually every sanctuary manager I talked with saw threats on the horizon, from global warming, which bleaches coral reefs, to the draining and channeling of the Everglades, which has forced wood storks to abandon their traditional nesting sites in Cork-screw Swamp. The overharvesting of horseshoe crabs at Cape May and the poaching of precious oyamel trees in El Rosario Monarch Butterfly Preserve are serious problems, too. But on the whole, habitat and wildlife are better protected here than they are in less-developed countries on other continents.

Thus, confining my visits to North America and to wildlife sanctuaries yielded a far more optimistic view of the prospects for wildlife than the standard model of looming ecological disaster. And that suggests an important message. Habitat and wildlife can be saved or restored, and sanctuary managers across North America are proving it every day.

Their efforts have paid big dividends. Bison now graze the Okla-homa grasslands at Tallgrass Prairie Preserve, where there were none a century ago; thousands of tundra swans winter at Lake Mattamuskeet, where farmers once planted corn; and the Mississippi Valley population of Canada geese has been brought back from the minuscule numbers of the 1930s to over one million birds, thanks to several midwestern water-fowl refuges. The managers of these sanctuaries have seen what can be done even with beat-up land, and they are, as one might expect, hopeful about the future of wildlife.

The field of ecology that stimulated concern about extinctions was island biogeography. In their groundbreaking book, *The Theory of Island Biogeography*, MacArthur and Wilson pointed out that habitats are being fragmented into "islands." The theory predicted that small islands would support fewer species than large ones. Ecologists were quick to realize the implications for wildlife sanctuaries. This led to the SLOSS debate, the disagreement among ecologists about sanctuary size.

No one disputes that large sanctuaries are preferable to small ones. But that begs the real questions that face the managers of public and private sanctuaries. Namely, are small sanctuaries important to wildlife? Are they worth the time and money required to maintain them, or should land managers concentrate their limited resources on fewer but larger sanctuaries?

Two considerations lead me to conclude that small preserves are important to wildlife.

The first concerns the impact of size on biodiversity. Although large natural areas contain more species than smaller areas of similar habitat (as predicted by island biogeography), this is only a local measure of biodiversity. Several small sanctuaries may contribute more to worldwide biodiversity than a larger one because they harbor endemic or rare species. Without the diminutive National Key Deer refuge in southern Florida, for example, Key deer would almost certainly be extinct.

The second reason for maintaining small refuges is equally important. During certain periods of their lives, some animals congregate in huge numbers in small areas—on their breeding or wintering grounds or in staging areas. Those places desperately need protection. If the tiny portions of Mexico's oyamel forests that shelter the entire wintering population of eastern monarch butterflies were destroyed, 100 million butterflies would be at risk. If the Canadian Wildlife Service eliminated its protection of fifteen-acre Machias Seal Island, the ten thousand birds that breed there might disappear. And if the short segment of Delaware Bay shoreline where hordes of horseshoe crabs lay their eggs weren't protected, hundreds of thousands of shorebirds might not find the food they need to finish their northward migrations.

In none of these cases would a species be threatened. The western population of monarchs, which winters in California, would be unaffected. Puffins would still breed north of Machias. And shorebirds would become less abundant but not extinct. Nevertheless, if the small sanctuaries that protect these creatures were not there, the loss of wildlife would be significant. And as a confirmed biophile, I think all wildlife adds meaning and pleasure to our lives.

Which brings us back to humans. What can we do to prevent the destruction of the world's ecosystems and wildlife? The root cause of the problem, as so many have pointed out, is human population growth. But besides controlling our reproductive urges and promoting Planned Parenthood and similar organizations, can we do anything else? I believe we can, and so do others.

E. O. Wilson, ahead of the crowd as usual, presented a well-thought-out list of things we should do to preserve what remains of the earth's biological diversity.

1. Survey the world's fauna and flora. Let's find out what's there by conducting field surveys of the hot spots of biological diversity.

2. Create biological wealth. Let's determine the economic value of those plants and animals in a natural community that may be used as food, in medicines, or for purposes of recreation.

3. Promote sustainable development. The poor people of Third World countries must often destroy the environment that supports them in order to survive. Let's help them develop sustainable ways of making a living.

4. Save what remains. Let's expand the amount of land devoted to nature preserves.

5. Restore the wildlands.

Each item in this list is important, but the last two may be the most important. The abundance of wildlife in the sanctuaries I visited indicates that some North American and Caribbean countries are doing a good job of protecting and restoring natural areas. The United States protects 11 percent of its land. In Canada, the figure is 8 percent. Compare these numbers with those of India, which protects 4.5 percent of its land, and Brazil, which protects less than 4 percent. But before we North Americans congratulate ourselves too vigorously, we should realize that we can do more. New Zealand protects 23 percent of its land, as does Austria, and both countries are prosperous.

More protected areas will help preserve the world's wildlife and biodiversity. Of course, preserving land means managing it. When we are lucky enough to acquire a more-or-less undisturbed wilderness, its management might consist only of protecting the land and its inhabitants. But we shouldn't limit acquisition programs to pristine properties; as we have seen, even degraded ecosystems can be restored. Horicon Marsh was so befouled by years of mismanagement that it wasn't even a marsh when state and federal governments bought it. But through the efforts of wildlife managers, it is now a highly productive waterfowl area. Restoring ecosystems, however, is not always practical or even possible. And it is always more expensive than protecting them before they are degraded. So acquiring undisturbed areas should be the top priority.

But even if we can acquire undisturbed lands and restore others, even if the percentage of the earth's protected land rises from approximately 6 percent today to double or even triple that, we will not be out of the woods. Global warming will bleach coral reefs no matter how many marine parks we create; acid rain will devastate spruce forests regardless of how well we guard the boundaries; and exotic pests will continue to kill Fraser firs as surely as an imported blight destroyed North America's once-widespread chestnuts.

Unfortunately, protecting and properly managing land is not a panacea for all that ails the world. And that brings us back to Professor Wilson's list of what should be done to preserve biodiversity. We should add one item to it: We need strong and vigorously enforced environmental laws. And because carbon dioxide, pollution, and exotics don't stop at national borders, they must be global laws.

Progress has already been made in one area. The agreement that led 130 nations to ban chlorofluorocarbons appears to be working. The worldwide production of those chemicals has almost stopped. Atmospheric chlorine, the by-product of CFCs that destroys ozone, is leveling off. In a few decades, the ozone layer may return to its normal thickness. And if we can accomplish that feat, it's not too much of a stretch to imagine the countries of the world taking on acid rain or global warming.

Passing laws, however, is the work of politicians, lawyers, and lobbyists. Conservationists should support their efforts, just as we support organizations and governments working to control population growth. But the negotiations are tedious, the results abstract. Many of us would prefer to help the environment in more concrete ways as well.

My travels convinced me that protecting land is the way to conserve wildlife and biodiversity. We must use our votes, our voices, and our money to encourage governments and nonprofit organizations—The Nature Conservancy, the National Audubon Society, and the myriad land trusts springing up come to mind—to set aside more land. North American wildlife managers have produced spectacular results on protected lands. Every acre we set aside will benefit the world's ecosystems, wildlife, and biodiversity.

Wildlife and biodiversity are truly the miners' canary. If they are healthy, so shall we be healthy. We North Americans can be proud of what we have accomplished; the abundance of Canada geese, monarch butterflies, and pronghorns bears good tidings about the state of the continent we inhabit. We can and should set aside more land—create more islands of hope. But it is at least as important that we help other countries on other continents do the same. When it comes to biodiversity, we are all in this together.

$\mathscr{A}$cknowledgments

I am grateful to Diane Manning, who did the cover drawings for the book, reviewed each chapter and accompanied me to many of the sanctuaries. Without her, this book—and every other one I've written—would not exist.

Two old friends, Martha and Jim Foght, kindly invited us to Bonaire, furnished us palatial quarters, and introduced us to that island's spectacular coral reefs. Thanks.

If there is a better organization for a writer to work with than John F. Blair, I haven't heard of it. Carolyn Sakowski and her staff know the publishing business, and it is a pleasure to watch them make books out of manuscripts. Steve Kirk's editorial suggestions were, as usual, gently offered and always on the mark.

I drew heavily on the experience and knowledge of several professional ecologists. Professors Haven Wiley and Peter White of the University of North Carolina at Chapel Hill read and critiqued parts of the book, and Dr. Johnny Randall of the North Carolina Botanical Garden patiently answered my questions and gave his opinion on a variety of subjects.

The men and women who run North America's wildlife sanctuaries generously shared their time and knowledge with me in long interviews, both in the office and in the field. They straightened me out on everything from evolutionary biology to how to identify obscure species of algae, even though they had to work doubly hard to keep up with their paying jobs. Many of them read and offered advice on parts of the book, and they introduced me to local experts who chipped in their own experiences and information. They all have my respect and gratitude. The following list of people who provided on-site assistance is as complete as an imperfect memory can make it. My thanks go to Kalli De Meyer, Shannon Ludwig, Ed Carlson, Laura Snook, Lincoln Brower, Bruce Luebke, Eric Schrading, Colin McKinnon, Jason Hudson, Kelly Davis, John Stanton, Dennis Luszcz, Bob Hamilton, Bena Little Bear, Tory Roberts, Mike Dunbar, Joy Belsky, Mike Nunn, Sam Pearsall, Jack Friend, Katrina Davis, Patti Meyers, Diane Penttila, Bill Wheeler, and Larry Vine.

Some people measure their wealth in dollars, others in the number of cows or seashells they own. In my family, we measure it by the number and the quality of the books in our library. I used many of those volumes while researching this book, but I consulted two of them regularly. E. O. Wilson's *The Diversity of Life* and David Quammen's *The Song of the Dodo* stimulated my thinking and provided valuable insights into the worldwide conservation effort. Their presence on my shelves enriches me, and I heartily recommend both.

Finally, though many people helped in the preparation of this book, the opinions expressed here are my own, and I am solely responsible for any omissions and errors that remain.

or More Information

Bonaire Marine Park
P.O. Box 368
Bonaire, Netherlands Antilles
(011) 599-7-8444

Corkscrew Swamp Sanctuary
375 Sanctuary Road
Naples, Fla. 33964
(941) 348-9143

Mexico Ministry of Tourism
(800) 44-MEXICO

Cape May National Wildlife Refuge
24 Kimbles Beach Road
Cape May Court House, N.J.
  08210-2078
(609) 463-0944

Canadian Wildlife Service,
  Atlantic Region
P.O. Box 6227
17 Waterfowl Lane
Sackville, New Brunswick E4L 1G6
(506) 364-5016

Mattamuskeet National
  Wildlife Refuge
Route 1, Box N-2
Swan Quarter, N.C. 27885
(252) 926-4021

Tallgrass Prairie Preserve
P.O. Box 458
Pawhuska, Okla. 74056
(918) 287-4803

Hart Mountain National
  Antelope Refuge
P.O. Box 111
Lakeview, Ore. 97630
(541) 947-3315

Bon Secour National
  Wildlife Refuge
12295 State Highway 180
Gulf Shores, Ala. 36547
(334) 540-7720

Horicon National Wildlife Refuge
W4279 Headquarters Road
Mayville, Wis. 53050
(920) 387-2658

Bibliography

Introduction
Wildlife Conservation in North America

Brooks, Paul. 1980. *Speaking for Nature: How Literary Naturalists from Henry Thoreau to Rachel Carson Have Shaped America*. Reprint. San Francisco: Sierra Club Books, 1983.

Diamond, Jared M. 1975. "The Island Dilemma: Lessons of Modern Biogeographic Studies for the Design of Natural Reserves." *Biological Conservation* 7: 129–46.

Elton, Charles. 1927. *Animal Ecology*. New York: Macmillan. Reprint with minor revisions. New York: October House, 1966.

Foster, Janet. 1998. *Working for Wildlife: The Beginning of Preservation in Canada*. 2nd ed. Toronto: University of Toronto Press.

Graham, Frank, Jr., with Carl W. Buchheister. 1990. *The Audubon Ark: A History of the National Audubon Society*. New York: Alfred A. Knopf. Reprint. Austin: University of Texas Press, 1992.

Laycock, George. 1973. *The Sign of the Flying Goose: The Story of the National Wildlife Refuges*. Rev. ed. Garden City, N.Y.: Anchor Press.

MacArthur, Robert H., and Edward O. Wilson. 1967. *The Theory of Island Biogeography*. Princeton, N.J.: Princeton University Press.

Matthiessen, Peter. 1987. *Wildlife in America*. 2nd ed. New York: Viking.

Noss, Reed F., and Allen Y. Cooperrider. 1994. *Saving Nature's Legacy: Protecting and Restoring Biodiversity*. Washington: Island Press.

Pearson, T. Gilbert. 1937. *Adventures in Bird Protection*. New York: Appleton Century Company.

Quammen, David. 1996. *The Song of the Dodo: Island Biogeography in an Age of Extinctions*. New York: Scribner.

———. 1998. "Planet of Weeds." *Harper's Magazine*, October 1998.

Simberloff, Daniel S., and Lawrence G. Abele. 1976. "Island Biogeographic Theory and Conservation Practice." *Science* 191: 285–86.

Simonian, Lane. 1995. *Defending the Land of the Jaguar: A History of Conservation in Mexico*. Austin: University of Texas Press.

Soulé, Michael E., and Bruce A. Wilcox, eds. 1980. *Conservation Biology: An Evolutionary-Ecological Perspective*. Sunderland, Mass.: Sinauer Associates.

Verney, Peter. 1979. *Animals in Peril: Man's War against Wildlife*. Provo, Utah: Brigham Young University Press.

Wilson, Edward O. 1992. *The Diversity of Life*. Cambridge, Mass.: Harvard University Press.

————. 1994. *Naturalist*. Washington: Island Press.

Worster, Donald. 1994. *Nature's Economy: A History of Ecological Ideas*. 2nd ed. Cambridge, England: Cambridge University Press.

Chapter 1
A Perfect Park

Ariyoshi, Rita. 1997. "Halting a Coral Catastrophe." *Nature Conservancy*, January/February 1997.

Bischof, Barbie. 1997. "Cities beneath the Sea." *Natural History*, December 1997/January 1998.

————. 1997. "Reefs in Crisis." *Natural History*, December 1997/January 1998.

Brown, Barbara E., and John C. Ogden. 1993. "Coral Bleaching." *Scientific American*, January 1993.

Bruckner, Andrew W., and Robin J. Bruckner. 1997. "Emerging Infections on the Reef." *Natural History*, December 1997/January 1998.

Dubinsky, Z., ed. 1990. *Ecosystems of the World*. Vol. 25. Amsterdam, Netherlands: Elsevier Science Publishers B.V.

Fagerstrom, J. A. 1987. *The Evolution of Reef Communities*. New York: John Wiley & Sons.

Glynn, P. W. 1990. "Feeding Ecology of Selected Coral-Reef Macroconsumers: Patterns and Effects on Coral Community Structure." In Dubinsky 1990.

————. 1997. "Requiem for Reefs?" *International Wildlife*, March/April 1997.

Hof, Tom van't. 1983. *Guide to the Bonaire Marine Park*. Curaçao, Netherlands Antilles: Orphan Publishing Company.

Kaplan, Eugene H. 1982. *A Field Guide to Coral Reefs: Caribbean and Florida*. Boston: Houghton Mifflin Company.

Logan, Brian W. 1961. "Cryptozoon and Associated Stromatolites from the Recent, Shark Bay, Western Australia." *Journal of Geology* 69: 517–33.

Logan, Brian W., Paul Hoffman, and Conrad D. Gebelein. 1974. "Algal Mats, Cryptalgal Fabrics, and Structures, Hamelin Pool, Western Australia." *American Association of Petroleum Geologists*, memoir 22: 140–94.

Pendick, Daniel. 1994. "Coral Reefs: Why So Rich?" *Earth*, September 1994.

Raup, David M. 1991. *Extinction: Bad Genes or Bad Luck?* New York: W. W. Norton & Company.

Schnabel, Jerry, and Susan L. Swygert. 1991. *Diving and Snorkeling Guide to Bonaire*. Houston, Tex.: Pisces Books.

Schopf, J. William, ed. 1992. *Major Events in the History of Life*. Boston: Jones and Bartlett Publishers.

Shultz, Leonard P. 1958. *Review of the Parrotfishes Family Scaridae*. Washington: Smithsonian Institution, United States National Museum Bulletin 214.

Stolzenburg, William. 1996. "Building a Better Refuge." *Nature Conservancy*, January/February 1996.

Wilson, Edward O. 1992. *The Diversity of Life*. Cambridge, Mass.: Harvard University Press.

Yamaguchi, M. 1986. "*Acanthaster planci* Infestations of Reefs and Coral Assemblies." *Coral Reefs* 5: 23–30.

Yonge, C. M. 1930. *A Year on the Great Barrier Reef*. New York: Putnam.

Chapter 2
Ancient Cypresses, Young Storks

Bent, Arthur Cleveland. 1926. *Life Histories of North American Marsh Birds*. Washington: Smithsonian Institution, United States National Museum Bulletin 135. Reprint. New York: Dover, 1963.

Blake, Nelson Manfred. 1980. *Land into Water—Water into Land: A History of Water Management in Florida*. Tallahassee: University Press of Florida.

Brevard, Caroline Mays. 1925. *A History of Florida from the Treaty of 1763 to Our Own Times*. Volume 2. Edited by James Alexander Robertson. Deland, Fla.: Florida State Historical Society.

Douglas, Marjory Stoneman. 1947. *The Everglades: River of Grass*. New York: Rinehart and Company. Reprinted with author's afterword. St. Simons Island, Ga.: Mockingbird Books, 1974.

Graham, Frank, Jr., with Carl W. Buchheister. 1990. *The Audubon Ark: A History of the National Audubon Society*. New York: Alfred A. Knopf. Reprint. Austin: University of Texas Press, 1992.

Hancock, J. A., J. A. Kushlan, and M. P. Kahl. 1992. *Storks, Ibises, and Spoonbills of the World*. London: Academic Press.

Kahl, M. P. 1964. "Food Ecology of the Wood Stork (*Mycteria americana*) in Florida." *Ecological Monographs* 34: 97–117.

Kushlan, James A., and Paula C. Frohring. 1986. "The History of the Southern Florida Wood Stork Population." *Wilson Bulletin* 98: 368–86.

Lodge, Thomas E. 1994. *The Everglades Handbook: Understanding the Ecosystem*. Delray Beach, Fla.: St. Lucie Press.

Manning, Phillip. 1997. *Orange Blossom Trails: Walks in the Natural Areas of Florida*. Winston-Salem, N.C.: John F. Blair, Publisher. This book contains a complete account of a walk in Corkscrew Swamp.

Ogden, John C., and Stephen A. Nesbitt. 1979. "Recent Wood Stork Population Trends." *Wilson Bulletin* 91: 512–23.

Proby, Kathryn Hall. 1974. *Audubon in Florida*. Miami, Fla.: University of Miami Press.

Proctor, Samuel. 1950. *Napoleon Bonaparte Broward: Florida's Fighting Democrat*. Gainesville: University of Florida Press.

Smith, Buckingham. 1869. "Will of Buckingham Smith." A copy of Smith's will was furnished by James G. Cusick, curator of the P. K. Yonge Library of Florida History, University of Florida, Gainesville.

———. 1911. "Report of Buckingham Smith, Esq., on His Reconnaissance of the Everglades 1848." *Everglades of Florida, Acts, Reports and Other Papers State and National, Relating to the Everglades of the State of Florida*. Washington: Senate Document 89: 46–55.

Smith, Buckingham, translator. 1866. *Narratives of the career of Hernando de Soto in the conquest of Florida, as told by a knight of Elvas, and in a relation by Luys Hernandez de Biedma, factor of the expedition*. Reprinted with an introduction by Edward Gaylord Bourne. New York: Allerton Book Company, 1922.

Stroud, Richard H., ed. 1985. *National Leaders of American Conservation*. Washington: Smithsonian Institution Press.

Terres, John K. 1991. *The Audubon Society Encyclopedia of American Birds*. New York: Wings Books. An earlier edition of this book was published by Alfred A. Knopf.

United States Fish and Wildlife Service. 1997. *Revised Recovery Plan for the U.S. Breeding Population of the Wood Stork*. Atlanta: United States Fish and Wildlife Service, Southeast Region.

Walker, R. J. 1911. "Extracts from the Instructions to Buckingham Smith, Esq., by the Secretary of the Treasury." *Everglades of Florida, Acts, Reports and Other Papers State and National, Relating to the Everglades of the State of Florida*. Washington: Senate Document 89: 37–38.

Chapter 3
Where Butterflies Go

Anderson, J. B., and L. P. Brower. 1996. "Freeze Protection of Overwintering Monarch Butterflies in Mexico: Critical Role of the Forest As a Blanket and an Umbrella." *Ecological Entomology* 21: 107–16.

Borkin, Susan Sullivan. 1993. "Rejection of *Apocynum androsaemifolium* and *A. sibricum* (Apocynaceae) As Food Plants by Larvae of *Danaus plexippus*: Refutation of Early Accounts." In Malcolm and Zalucki 1993.

Brower, Lincoln P. 1977. "Monarch Migration." *Natural History*, June/July 1977.

———. 1995. "Understanding and Misunderstanding the Migration of the Monarch Butterfly (Nymphalidae) in North America." *Journal of the Lepidopterists' Society* 48: 304–85.

———. 1996. "Monarch Butterfly Orientation: Missing Pieces of a Magnificent Puzzle." *Journal of Experimental Biology* 199: 93–103.

Carlson, Shawn. 1997. "Unraveling the Secrets of the Monarchs." *Scientific American*, September 1997.

Castilla, Susana Rojas Gonzalez de. 1993. "The Importance of Alternative Sources of Income to 'Ejidatarios' (Local Residents) for Conservation of Overwintering Areas of the Monarch Butterfly." In Malcolm and Zalucki 1993.

Coffey, Timothy. 1993. *The History and Folklore of North American Wildflowers*. Boston: Houghton Mifflin Company.

Fabre, Jean Henri. 1991. *The Insect World of J. Henri Fabre.* Translated by Alexander Teixeira de Mattos. Boston: Beacon Press. This book is a collection of Fabre's writings, which were originally published as a ten-volume set entitled *Souvenirs Entomologiques,* the last volume of which appeared in 1907.

Fehrenbach, T. R. 1995. *Fire and Blood: A History of Mexico.* Rev. ed. New York: Da Capo Press.

Grace, Eric S. 1997. *The World of the Monarch Butterfly.* San Francisco: Sierra Club Books.

Grieve, M. 1931. *A Modern Herbal.* Vol. 1. New York: Harcourt, Brace & Company.

James, Wilma Robert. 1973. *Know Your Poisonous Plants.* Healdsburg, Calif.: Naturegraph Publishers.

Lewis, Walter H. 1977. *Medical Botany: Plants Affecting Man's Health.* New York: John Wiley & Sons.

Malcolm, Stephen B. 1993. "Conservation of Monarch Butterfly Migration in North America: An Endangered Phenomenon." In Malcolm and Zalucki 1993.

Malcolm, Stephen B., and Myron P. Zalucki. 1993. *Biology and Conservation of the Monarch Butterfly.* Los Angeles: Natural History Museum of Los Angeles County.

Snook, Laura C. 1993. "Conservation of the Monarch Butterfly Reserves in Mexico: Focus on the Forest." In Malcolm and Zalucki 1993.

Urquhart, Fred A. 1976. "Found at Last: The Monarch's Winter Home." *National Geographic,* August 1976.

———. 1987. *The Monarch Butterfly: International Traveler.* Chicago: Nelson-Hall.

Woodson, R. E., Jr. 1954. "The North American Species *Asclepias.*" *Annals of the Missouri Botanical Garden* 41: 1–211.

Young, Allen M. 1982. "An Evolutionary-Ecological Model for the Evolution of Migratory Behavior in the Monarch Butterfly, and Its Absence in the Queen Butterfly." *Acta Biotheoretica* 31: 219–37.

Chapter 4
Shorebirds and Crabs

Burger, Joanna. 1996. *A Naturalist along the Jersey Shore.* New Brunswick, N.J.: Rutgers University Press.

Castro, Gonzalo, and J. P. Myers. 1993. "Shorebird Predation on Eggs of Horseshoe Crabs during Spring Stopover on Delaware Bay." *The Auk* 110: 927–30.

Castro, Gonzalo, J. P. Myers, and Allen R. Place. 1989. "Assimilation Efficiency of Sanderlings (*Calidris alba*) Feeding on Horseshoe Crab (*Limulus polyphemus*) Eggs." *Physiological Zoology* 62: 716–31.

Clark, Kathleen E., and Lawrence J. Niles. 1993. "Abundance and Distribution of Migrant Shorebirds in Delaware Bay." *The Condor* 95: 694–705.

Connor, Jack. 1991. *Season at the Point*. New York: Atlantic Monthly Press.

Dunne, P., D. Sibley, C. Sutton, and W. Wander. 1982. "1982 Aerial Shorebird Survey of Delaware Bay." *Records of New Jersey Birds* 8: 68–75.

Harrington, Brian. 1982. "Untying the Enigma of the Red Knot." *Living Bird Quarterly*, Autumn 1982.

Harrington, Brian, with Charles Flowers. 1996. *The Flight of the Red Knot*. New York: W. W. Norton & Company.

Harriot, Thomas. 1590. *A Briefe and True Report of the New Found Land of Virginia*. Reprint. New York: Dover, 1972.

Milne, Lorus, and Margery Milne. 1967. *The Crab That Crawled out of the Past*. New York: Atheneum.

Minton, Clive. 1997. "Mean Weight of Red Knots on Delaware Bay 16–26 May 1997." Unpublished data from the Pleasantville, New Jersey, office of the United States Fish and Wildlife Service.

Myers, J. P. 1986. "Sex and Gluttony on Delaware Bay." *Natural History*, May 1986.

National Audubon Society. 1997. "Crash of Shorebird Population Linked to Overfishing of Horseshoe Crabs." *National Audubon Society Action Alert!* July 17, 1997.

Novitsky, Thomas J. 1984. "Discovery to Commercialization: The Blood of the Horseshoe Crab." *Oceanus* 27: 13–18.

Sargent, William. 1987. *The Year of the Crab*. New York: W. W. Norton & Company.

Shuster, Carl N., and Mark L. Botton. 1985. "A Contribution to the Population Biology of Horseshoe Crabs, *Limulus polyphemus* (L.), in Delaware Bay." *Estuaries* 8: 363–72.

Stone, Witmer. 1937. *Bird Studies at Old Cape May*. New York: Dover.

Tsipoura, Nellie, and Joanna Burger. 1998. "Shorebird Diet during Spring Migration Stopover on Delaware Bay." Unpublished paper.

Williams, Henry Smith. 1904. *The Historians' History of the World*. Vol. 18. New York: Outlook Company.

Chapter 5
The Surviving Auk

Audubon, Maria R., and Elliott Coues. 1898. *Audubon and His Journals*. Vol. 1. London: John C. Nimmo.

Bent, Arthur Cleveland. 1919. *Life Histories of North American Diving Birds*. Washington: Smithsonian Institution, United States National Museum Bulletin 107.

Blake, B. F. 1984. "Diet and Fish Stock Availability as Possible Factors in the Mass Death of Auks in the North Sea." *Journal of Experimental Marine Biology and Ecology* 76: 89–103.

Conkling, Philip W., ed. 1995. *From Cape Cod to the Bay of Fundy: An Environmental Atlas of the Gulf of Maine*. Cambridge, Mass.: MIT Press.

Eckert, Allan W. 1963. *The Great Auk*. New York: Little, Brown and Company.

Evans, Peter G. H., and David N. Nettleship. 1985. "Conservation of the Atlantic Alcidae." In Nettleship and Birkhead 1985.

Kunzig, Robert. 1995. "Twilight of the Cod." *Discover*, April 1995.

MacKinnon, C. M., and A. D. Smith. 1985. *A Summary of Historical Information on the Seabirds of Machias Seal Island*. Sackville, New Brunswick: Canadian Wildlife Service.

Montevecchi, Bill. 1994. "The Great Auk Cemetery." *Natural History*, August 1994.

Nettleship, David N., and Tim R. Birkhead. 1985. *The Atlantic Alcidae*. New York: Academic Press.

Nettleship, David N., and Peter G. H. Evans. 1985. "Distribution and Status of the Atlantic Alcidae." In Nettleship and Birkhead 1985.

Platt, John F., and David N. Nettleship. 1985. "Diving Depths of Four Alcids." *The Auk* 102: 293–97.

Silverberg, Robert. 1967. *The Auk, the Dodo, and the Oryx: Vanished and Vanishing Creatures*. New York: Thomas Y. Crowell.

Stolzenburg, William. 1997. "Habitat Is Where It's At." *Nature Conservancy*, November/December 1997.

Wanless, S., J. A. Morris, and M. P. Harris. 1988. "Diving Behavior of Guillemot *Uria aalge*, Puffin *Fratercula arctica* and razorbill *Alca torda* as Shown by Radiotelemetry." *Journal of Zoology, London* 216: 73–81.

Chapter 6
Goose Lake, Swan Lake

Baldassarre, Guy A., and Eric G. Bolen. 1994. *Waterfowl Ecology and Management*. New York: John Wiley & Sons.

Begon, Michael, John L. Harper, and Colin R. Townsend. 1990. *Ecology: Individuals, Populations and Communities*. Boston: Blackwell Scientific Publications.

Bellrose, Frank C. 1976. *Ducks, Geese and Swans of North America*. Harrisburg, Pa.: Stackpole Books.

Colinvaux, Paul. 1978. *Why Big Fierce Animals Are Rare. An Ecologist's Perspective*. Princeton, N.J.: Princeton University Press.

Dudley, Jack. 1995. *Mattamuskeet and Ocracoke Waterfowl Heritage*. Morehead City, N.C.: Coastal Heritage Series.

Elton, Charles. 1927. *Animal Ecology*. New York: Macmillan. Reprint with minor revisions. New York: October House, 1966.

Forest, Lewis C. 1988. "An Overview of the History of Mattamuskeet Drainage District and the Efforts by Private Corporations to Reclaim the Lands under the Waters of Lake Mattamuskeet for Productive Agricultural Purposes." In *Lake Mattamuskeet Lodge: Recommendations for Adaptive Reuse*. Greenville, N.C.: East Carolina University Regional Development Institute.

Grinnell, Joseph. 1917. "Field Test of Theories Concerning Distributional Control." *American Naturalist* 51: 115–28.

———. 1924. "Geography and Evolution." *Ecology* 5: 225–29.

———. 1928. "Presence and Absence of Animals." *University of California Chronicles* 30: 429–50.

Hardy, Alister. 1968. "Charles Elton's Influence in Ecology." *Journal of Animal Ecology* 37: 3–8.

Hindman, Larry J., and Vernon D. Stotts. 1982. "Chesapeake Bay and North Carolina Sounds." In Weller 1982.

Odum, Eugene P. 1971. *Fundamentals of Ecology*. 3rd ed. Philadelphia: W. B. Saunders Company.

Stewart, Doug. 1993. "No Honking Matter." *National Wildlife*, December 1992/January 1993: 40–43.

Vandermeer, J. H. 1972. "Niche Theory." *Annual Review of Ecology and Systematics* 3: 107–32.

Venters, Vic. 1991. "No Sad Songs for Swans." *Wildlife in North Carolina*, December 1991.

——. 1996. "Canadas in Crisis." *Wildlife in North Carolina*, November 1996.

Weller, Milton, ed. 1982. *Waterfowl in Winter*. Lubbock, Tex.: Texas Tech University Press.

Wilson, Edward O. 1992. *The Diversity of Life*. Cambridge, Mass.: Harvard University Press.

Yelverton, Carl S., and Thomas L. Quay. 1959. *Food Habits of the Canada Goose at Lake Mattamuskeet, North Carolina*. Raleigh, N.C.: North Carolina Wildlife Resources Commission.

Chapter 7
Where the Buffalo Roam

Anderson, Elaine. 1984. "Who's Who in the Pleistocene." In Martin and Klein 1984.

Begon, Michael, John L. Harper, and Colin R. Townsend. 1990. *Ecology: Individuals, Populations and Communities*. 2nd ed. Boston: Blackwell Scientific Publications.

Benning, T. L. and Thomas B. Bragg. 1993. "Response of Big Bluestem (Andropogon gerardii Vitman) to Timing of Spring Burning." *American Midlands Naturalist* 130: 127–32.

Brown, Lauren. 1985. *Grasslands*. New York: Alfred A. Knopf.

Chase, Alston. 1987. *Playing God in Yellowstone: The Destruction of America's First National Park*. New York: Harcourt Brace Jovanovich.

Gard, Wayne. 1959. *The Great Buffalo Hunt*. New York: Alfred A. Knopf.

Hamilton, Bruce. 1994. "An Enduring Wilderness." *Sierra*, October 1994.

Kline, Virginia M. 1997. "Orchards of Oak and a Sea of Grass." In Packard and Mutel 1997.

Leopold, Aldo. 1949. *A Sand County Almanac*. New York: Oxford University Press.

Madson, John. 1982. *Where the Sky Began: Land of the Tallgrass Prairie*. Boston: Houghton Mifflin Company.

Manning, Phillip. 1997. *Orange Blossom Trails: Walks in the Natural Areas of Florida*. Winston-Salem, N.C.: John F. Blair, Publisher.

Manning, Richard. 1995. *Grassland*. New York: Penguin Books.

Martin, Paul S., and Richard G. Klein, eds. 1984. *Quaternary Extinctions: A Prehistoric Revolution*. Tucson: University of Arizona Press.

McPhee, John. 1986. *Rising from the Plains*. New York: Farrar, Straus, & Giroux.

Packard, Stephen, and Cornelia F. Mutel, eds. 1997. *The Tallgrass Restoration Handbook*. Washington: Island Press.

Pendick, Daniel. 1997. "Rocky Mountain Why." *Earth*, June 1997.

Shaw, Julie. 1998. *A Guide to The Nature Conservancy's Tallgrass Prairie Preserve*. Tulsa, Okla.: The Nature Conservancy.

Smith, Annick. 1996. *Big Bluestem: Journey into the Tallgrass*. Tulsa, Okla.: Council Oak Books.

West, Frederick Hadleigh, ed. 1996. *American Beginnings: The Prehistory and Paleoecology of Beringia*. Chicago: University of Chicago Press.

Woodburne, Michael O., ed. 1987. *Cenozoic Animals of North America: Geochronology and Biostratigraphy*. Berkeley: University of California Press.

Chapter 8
The Antelope Dilemma

Ambrose, Stephen E. 1996. *Undaunted Courage: Meriwether Lewis, Thomas Jefferson, and the Opening of the American West*. New York: Simon & Schuster.

Audubon, John James. 1842–46. *Viviparous Quadrupeds of North America*. Reprint. *Audubon's Quadrupeds of North America*. Secaucus, N.J.: Wellfleet Press, 1989.

Brown, Lauren. 1985. *Grasslands*. New York: Alfred A. Knopf.

Byers, John A. 1998. *American Pronghorn*. Chicago: University of Chicago Press.

Derr, Mark. 1994. "Growing Bigger Coyotes." *Audubon*, November/December 1994.

Durham, Michael S. 1997. *Desert between the Mountains: Mormons, Miners, Padres, Mountain Men, and the Opening of the Great Basin, 1772–1869*. New York: Henry Holt and Company.

Einarsen, Arthur. 1948. *The Pronghorn Antelope and Its Management*. Washington: Wildlife Management Institute.

Fradkin, Philip L. 1989. *Sagebrush Country: Land and the American West*. New York: Alfred A. Knopf.

Harper, Kimball T., Larry L. St. Clair, Kaye H. Thorne, and Wilford M. Hess, eds. 1994. *Natural History of the Colorado Plateau and Great Basin*. Niwot, Colo.: University Press of Colorado.

Kittredge, William. 1992. *A Hole in the Sky: A Memoir*. New York: Alfred A. Knopf.

Lee, Raymond M., James D. Yoakum, Bart W. O'Gara, Thomas M. Pojar, and

Richard A. Ockenfels, eds. 1998. *Pronghorn Management Guides: Eighteenth Biennial Pronghorn Antelope Workshop*. Prescott, Ariz.: Arizona Antelope Foundation.

Leydet, François. 1988. *The Coyote: Defiant Songdog of the West*. Rev. ed. Norman, Okla.: University of Oklahoma Press.

MacMahon, James A. 1985. *Deserts*. New York: Alfred A. Knopf.

Matthiessen, Peter. 1987. *Wildlife in America*. Rev. ed. New York: Viking.

McPhee, John. 1980. *Basin and Range*. New York: Farrar, Straus, & Giroux.

Peterson, David. 1994. "The Killing Fields." *Wilderness*, Summer 1994.

Turbak, Gary. 1995. *Pronghorn: Portrait of the American Antelope*. Flagstaff, Ariz.: Northland Publishing. The quote from Sergeant Ordway's journal was taken from this book.

Chapter 9
The Science of Muddling Through

Bent, Arthur Cleveland. 1953. *Life Histories of North American Wood Warblers*. Part 1. Smithsonian Institution, United States National Museum Bulletin 203. Reprint. New York: Dover, 1963.

Harrison, Hal H. 1984. *Wood Warblers' World*. New York: Simon & Schuster.

Morse, Douglass H. 1989. *American Warblers: An Ecological and Behavioral Perspective*. Cambridge, Mass.: Harvard University Press.

Pelikan, Matthew. 1996. "The Yellow-rumped Clan." *Birder's World*, June 1996.

Quammen, David. 1998. "Planet of Weeds." *Harper's Magazine*, October 1998.

Robinson, Scott K. 1996. "Nest Gains, Nest Losses." *Natural History*, July 1996.

Schorre, Barth. 1998. *The Wood Warblers*. Austin: University of Texas Press.

Service, Robert W. 1983. "The Cremation of Sam McGee." In *Robert W. Service: Best Tales of the Yukon*. Edited by Tam Mossman. Philadelphia: Running Press.

Terborgh, John. 1992. "Why American Songbirds Are Vanishing." *Scientific American*, May 1992.

Terrill, Scott B., and Robert L. Crawford. 1988. "Additional Evidence of Nocturnal Migration by Yellow-Rumped Warblers in Winter." *The Condor* 90: 261–63.

Terrill, Scott B., and Robert D. Ohmart. 1984. "Facultative Extension of Fall Migration by Yellow-Rumped Warblers (*Dendroica coronata*)." *The Auk* 101: 427–38.

Chapter 10
Where the Wild Goose Goes

Bellrose, Frank C. 1976. *Ducks, Geese and Swans of North America*. 2nd ed. Harrisburg, Pa.: Stackpole Books.

Craven, Scott R. 1984. "Fall Food Habits of Canada Geese in Wisconsin." *Journal of Wildlife Management* 48: 169–73.

Gard, Robert E. 1972. *Wild Goose Marsh: Horicon Stopover*. Madison: Wisconsin House.

Gilbert, Bil. 1977. "Uncle Sam Says Scram." *Audubon*, January 1977.

Leopold, Aldo. 1933. *Game Management*. Reprint. Madison: University of Wisconsin Press, 1986.

———. 1949. *A Sand County Almanac*. Reprint with some additions. *A Sand County Almanac: With Essays on Conservation from Round River*. New York: Ballantine Books, 1970.

Lorbiecki, Marybeth. 1996. *Aldo Leopold: A Fierce Green Fire*. Helena, Mont.: Falcon Publishing Company.

Manning, Phillip. 1995. *Palmetto Journal: Walks in the Natural Areas of South Carolina*. Winston-Salem, N.C.: John F. Blair, Publisher. This book contains an account of the introduction of carp in the United States.

Watkins, T. H. 1994. "The Hundred-Million-Acre Understanding." *Audubon*, September/October 1994.

Chapter 11
Putting It All Together

Eldredge, Niles. *Dominion*. New York: Henry Holt and Company.

MacArthur, Robert H., and Edward O. Wilson. 1967. *The Theory of Island Biogeography*. Princeton, N.J.: Princeton University Press.

Morell, Virginia. 1999. "The Variety of Life." *National Geographic*, February 1999.

Quammen, David. 1998. "Planet of Weeds." *Harper's Magazine*, October 1998.

United Nations. 1997. *Statistical Yearbook*. 42nd issue, 1995. New York: United Nations Publications.

Wilson, Edward O. 1992. *The Diversity of Life*. Cambridge, Mass.: Harvard University Press.

Zimmer, Carl. 1995. "Unintended Consequences." *Discover*, March 1995.

ℐndex

Abele, Lawrence, 9

Abies religiosa, 52. *See also* Oyamel

Academy of Natural Sciences of Philadelphia, 79

Adams, Kenneth and Diana, 125

Alca torda, 87. *See also* Razorbill

Alga, blue-green, 21 (*See also* Cyanobacteria); symbiotic, 20, 21

Amoco Cadiz, 93

American Midland Naturalist, 119

American Ornithologists' Union, 79

Andropogon, gerardi, 117. *See also* Bluestem, big

Angangueo, Mex., 50, 51

Angelfish, French, 22, 23

Animal Damage Control, 135

Animal Ecology, 5

Antelocapra americana, 131, 132. *See also* Pronghorn

Asclepias syriaca, 56. *See also* Milkweed, common

Atlantic Alcidae, The, 93

Atlantic Flyway Council, 110, 112

Atlantic States Marine Fisheries Commission, 73, 80, 82

Atseenahoofa, 31, 41. *See also* Big Cypress Swamp

Audubon, John James, 36, 88, 89, 135

Auk, great, 84, 85, 88, 97, 156

Auk, The, 79

Babbitt, Bruce, 121

Baker, John Hopkinson, 41, 42

Banff National Park, 4

Bang, Frederick, 72

Baraboo, Wis., 165, 174

Barnard Ranch, 115, 120, 121

Bellrose, Frank, 108

Belsky, Joy, 144-47

Bent, Arthur Cleveland, 35, 45, 89, 154

Big Bluestem, 119

Big Cypress Swamp, 41; proposal to drain, 31-34, 39; development in, 47

Bird Studies at Old Cape May, 79

Birkeland, Charles, 14

Bison bison, 118. *See also* Bison, plains

Bison latifrons, 118

Bison priscus. See Bison, steppe

Bison: plains, 118, 123-25, 133, 181; steppe, 118

Blackwater National Wildlife Refuge, 105

Blevins, Paul, 150, 155, 158

Bluestem, big, 117, 120, 125

Bluestem, little, 120, 125

Bonaire Marine Park, 10, 11-28

Bon Secour National Wildlife Refuge, 148

Boone and Crockett Club, 138

Botton, Mark L., 78, 81

Bradley, Guy, 39

Bradley, Nina Leopold, 175

Brandsson, Jon, 84

Branta canadensis, 106, 168. *See also* Goose, Canada

Briefe and True Report of the New Found Land

of *Virginia, A*, 71

Broward, Napoleon Bonaparte, 39, 40

Brower, Lincoln, 54, 64

Brown, Lauren, 119

Brugger, Cathy, 54, 56, 58

Brugger, Kenneth, 54, 56, 58

Burger, Joanna, 67, 78

Byers, John, 133, 146

Cabot, John, 88

Calidris canutus, 66. *See also* Knot, red.

Canadian Wildlife Service, 6, 86, 90, 95, 96, 182

Canis latrans, 134. *See also* Coyote

Canute, King, 66

Cape May National Wildlife Refuge, 65-82, 181

Cape May, N.J., 65, 66, 76, 79

Cardiac glycoside, 57, 58

Carlson, Ed, 42, 46, 47

Carp, 108, 171-74

Carson, Rachel, 6, 165

Castilla, Susana de, 64

Castro, Alejandro, 50, 51, 64

Castro, Gonzalo, 70

Cattails, 167, 168, 171-74

Celery, wild, 103, 107, 108

Charles Sheldon Wild Life Refuge, 138, 139

Chase, Alton, 128

Chesapeake Bay, 104, 105, 107-9

Chlorofluorocarbons (CFCs), 184, 185

Clark, Saterlee, 163

Clark, William, 132, 135

Collier County, Fla., 47

Collier Enterprises, 42

Connor, Jack, 76

Conservation biology: definition of, 8

Conservation Biology: An Ecological Perspective, 8

Coral, 20, 21, 23, 24; effect of rising sea levels on, 24, 25, 27, 28; elkhorn, 11, 12; golf-ball, 17; staghorn, 17; star, 17

Corkscrew Swamp, 41

Corkscrew Swamp Sanctuary, 30-48, 181

Cowbird, brown-headed, 152

Coyote, 131, 134-37, 139, 142-47, 153, 159

Cyanobacteria, 18, 19

Cygnus columbiana, 99. *See also* Swan, tundra

Danaus plexippus, 53. *See also* Monarch butterfly

Darling, Jay Norwood "Ding," 6

Darwin, Charles, 3

Davis, Katrina, 159, 160

Davis, Kelly, 104, 106-9

Delaware Bay, 65, 67-71, 73, 75, 76, 78, 81

Delaware Valley Ornithological Club, 79

Delmarva Peninsula, 104, 107-10

Dendroica coronata, 153. *See also* Warbler, yellow-rumped

Diadema antillarum. *See* Urchin, long-spined sea

Diamond, Jared, 8, 9

Diversity, biological: in tallgrass prairie, 124, 126; loss of, 156, 178-80; preservation of, 183-85

Diversity of Life, The, 112

Donne, John, 48

Douglas, Marjory Stoneman, 35

Ducks, populations of at Horicon Marsh, 168, 171, 172

Ducks, Geese & Swans of North America, 108

Dunbar, Mike, 141, 142

Dunne, Pete, 67, 76

Ecological Society of America, 121

Ecology, 100

Ecology, restoration, 120, 121

Edison, Thomas, 56

Einarsen, Arthur, 143

Ejido, 61-64

Eldridge, Niles, 179

Eleocharis parvula. See Spike rush, dwarf

Elk, 124, 127

Elk Village, 163

Eliot, Willard, 36

El Niño, 28

El Rosario Monarch Butterfly Preserve, 10, 49-64, 159

Elton, Charles, 5, 101

Endangered Species Act, 80

Endotoxin, bacterial, 72

Evans, Peter G.H., 93, 94

Everglades, 31-35, 180; proposal to drain, 31-34, 39

Everglades National Park, 42

Evolution: convergent, 85

Exotics, invasive, 127

Extinction, rates of, 178

Exxon Valdez, 93

Fabre, Jean Henri, 54, 55

Farragut, David, 151

Fehrenbach, T.R., 61

Field of Dreams, 159

Finger, Linda, 45

Fire: control of, 122, 123; deliberately set, 119, 121, 122; marsh, 164, 165; naturally occurring, 119, 120

Flint Hills, 115, 119, 120, 122, 127

Foght, Jim, 11

Foght, Martha, 11, 21

Fort Lauderdale, Fla., 40

Fort Morgan, 151, 152

Fratercula arctica, 87. *See also* Puffin, Atlantic

Frémont, John C., 136

Friend, Jack, 156-58, 160, 161

Friend, Venetia, 156, 157

Friends of Animals, 141

Game Management, 168, 174, 175

Gaynor, Richard, 157

Generalists, specialists competition with, 155, 156

Georges Bank, 71, 91

Global warming, 27, 28

Goose, Canada, 98-100, 102, 106, 107, 159, 176; differential survival of, 110-12; field feeding of 104; Mississippi Valley population of, 168-71, 181; shortstopping of, 105

Goose Wars, 169, 170

Grand Banks, 88, 91

Grass: Indian, 120; switch, 120

Great Basin, 136-37; stock grazing in, 138

Grasslands, 119

Great Auk, The, 84

Great Barrier Reef, 12, 26

Grinnell, Charles, 100, 101

Gulf of Maine, 95-97

Gulf of Mexico, 149, 150

Gulf Shores, Ala., 149, 156

Haeckel, Ernst, 5

Hamilton, Bob, 115, 116, 121, 122-24

Harrier, northern, 126

Harrington, Brian, 67, 70

Harriot, Thomas, 71

Hartline, H. Keffer, 80, 81

Hart Mountain, 137

Hart Mountain National Antelope Refuge, 130-47, 159, 166

Hecksher, Augustus, 100

Hixon, Mark, 17

Hole in the Sky, A, 139

Hoover Dike, 40

Horicon Lake, 163

Horicon Marsh: calling of Canada geese into, 168, 169; drainage of, 164, 165; formation of, 162, 163; reflooding of 167, 168; return of ducks to, 168; silting in of, 173, 174

Horicon National Wildlife Refuge, 162-76

Horseshoe crab, 65, 67-75, 75-82, 181, 182

Horseshoe Lake Refuge, 168

Hudson Bay, 68

Hudson, Jason, 90-92, 96

Hutchinson, G. Evelyn, 5

Island biogeography, principles of, 7-9

"Island Dilemma: Lessons of Modern Biogeographic Studies for the Design of Nature Reserves, The" 8, 9

Isleffson, Sigourour, 84

Izaak Walton League, 165

Johnson, Lyndon B., 167

Jonesport, Me., 83, 91, 95

Journal of Zoology, London, 88

Kahl, Philip, 38, 39

Kaibab Plateau, 128

Kimbles Beach, N.J., 69, 74, 77, 80

Kittelson, Ketil, 85

Kitteredge, William, 139

Klein Bonaire, 13

Knot, red, 65-67, 69, 79

Lakeview, Ore., 139

Lee Tidewater Cypress Company, 42

Leopold, Aldo, 113, 128, 165-67, 174-76

Lespedeza cuneata, 127

Levin, Jack, 72

Lewis and Clark Expedition, 119, 132, 135

Life and Death of Coral Reefs, 17

Life Histories of North American Marsh Birds, 35

Limulus amoebocyte lysate (LAL), 72, 73

Limulus polyphemus, 67, 68, 71, 82. *See also* Horseshoe crab

Logan, Brian, 18

Ludwig, Shannon, 43, 44, 46

Luebke, Bruce, 75-77, 80

Luszcz, Dennis, 107, 109, 110

MacArthur, Robert H., 7, 181

Machias Seal Island, 83-97, 182

Madrid, Miguel de la, 61

Malcolm, Stephen, 58

Mariposa Preserve, 6

Matinicus Rock, 4

Mattamuskeet, Lake, 98, 102, 107; history of 99-101

Mattamuskeet National Wildlife Refuge, 98-113, 159, 164, 181

McIntosh, Robert, 6

Meyer, Kalli De, 25-28, 62, 111

Meyers, Patti, 170-75

Migration: facultative, 154, 157; true, 154

Migratory Bird Treaty, 90

Milkweed, 56-58; common, 56

Millet, wild, 103

Miohippus, 117, 118

Mobile Bay, 149, 151, 152

Monarca, A.C., 63, 64

Monarch butterfly, 52-60, 150, 155, 182

Monarch Butterfly: International Traveler, The, 55

Muir, John, 4, 165

Muskgrass, 103, 107, 108

Mutel, Cornelia, 121

Mycteria americana, 34. *See also* stork, wood.

Myers, J.P., 70

National Audubon Society, 4, 10, 39, 41, 71, 138, 185

National Bison Range (Montana), 133, 146

National Wildlife Refuge System Improvement Act of 1997, 147

Nature Conservancy, The, 10, 76, 88, 93, 115, 116, 120, 121, 148, 158, 161, 185

Netherlands Antilles, 13

Nettleship, David N., 93, 94

New Jersey Audubon Society, 76

New Jersey Endangered and Nongame Species Program, 74

Niche, ecological, definition of, 100, 101

North Carolina Wildlife Resources Commission, 109

Norton, Barna B., 83, 85, 86, 94-96

Norton, John, 85

Nunn, Mike, 141, 145-47

Okeechobee, Lake, 34, 40

Oil spill, 93, 94

Olney's three-square, 103

Ordway, John, 132

Oregonian, 141

Oregon Natural Desert Association, 142, 144, 147

Osage County, Okla., 114, 115, 121

Osage Indians, 114

Owens, D.D., 124

Oyamel (fir), 52, 53, 60, 181, 182; protection of 60-64

Packard, Stephen, 121

Parrotfish, 15, 16; blue, 15; stoplight, 12; yellowtail, 15

Pawhuska, Okla., 114

Payne, Harvey, 115

Pearsall, Sam, 148, 149, 158, 161

Pearson, T. Gilbert, 41

Pelican Island, 4

Penttila, Diane, 171

Petrel, Leach's storm, 91

Phelps, F.N., 37

Phytoplankton, 19, 20

Pinchot, Gifford, 168

Pike, Northern, 163, 173

Pine Beach Trail, 149, 150

Pinguinus impennis, 85. See also Auk, great

Place, Allen R., 70

"Planet of Weeds," 156, 179

Playing God in Yellowstone, 128

Pocosin Lakes National Wildlife Refuge, 109

Prairie, shortgrass, 133; tallgrass, 114-29

Predator Defense Institute, 142

Pronghorn, 124, 130-34, 136-47, 159

Pronghorn Antelope and Its Management, The, 143

Protected areas, 159, 183, 184

Puffin, Atlantic, 86, 87, 90, 91, 95, 182

Quammen, David, 9, 156, 179

Radke, Louis "Curley," 165

Razorbill, 86, 87-93

Redhead Hiking Trail, 170

Coral reef: bleaching of, 26, destruction of, 12, 13; effect of rising sea levels on, 27, 28; preservation of, 14, 25-28

Roberts, Victoria, 139-42, 146, 147

Rock River, 162, 164, 173

Rocky Mountains: origins of, 116, 117

Roosevelt, Theodore, 4, 5, 165

Sand County Almanac, A, 128, 168, 175

Sanderling, 65, 70, 79

Sandpiper, semipalmated, 65, 79

Scarus coerleus, 15. See also Parrotfish, blue

Schultz, Leonard, 15

Schrading, Eric, 73-75, 78, 82

Season at the Point, 76

Shark, 22

Shark Bay, 18

Sheep, California bighorn, 159

Shuster, Carl N., 78, 81

Silent Spring, 6

Simberloff, Daniel, 9

SLOSS debate, 9, 84, 96, 97, 181, 182

Smith, Annick, 119

Smith, Thomas Buckingham, 30-34, 39, 44

Snook, Laura, 49, 50, 63

Song of the Dodo, The, 9

Soulé, Michael, 8

Spike rush, dwarf, 103

Starfish, crown-of-thorns, 12

Stanton, John, 102-6, 109

St. Augustine, Fla., 30, 31, 33

Stewart, Donal "Captain Don," 13

Stone, Witmer, 79

Stork, wood, 30, 34-39, 41-46, 181; population estimates of, 45, 46

Stromatolite, 18, 19

Sutton, Clay, 76

Swan, tundra, 99, 100-102; field feeding by 108, 109, 159

Tachypleus tridentatus, 81

Tallgrass Prairie Preserve, 114-29, 181

Tallgrass Restoration Handbook, The, 121

Tern, 92; arctic, 86, 90, 91; common, 91

Theory of Island Biogeography, The, 7, 181

Thoreau, Henry David, 3, 113

Tierra del Fuego, 66

Transverse Neovolcanic Belt, 58, 60

Tsipoura, Nellie, 77

Turnstone, ruddy, 65, 78, 79

Ungava Bay, Quebec, 110

United States Fish and Wildlife Service, 73, 75, 80, 141, 158-160, 171, 174, 179

Urchin, long-spined sea, 17

Urquhart, Fred, 54-56

Urquhart, Norah, 55

Vallisneria americanus. See Celery, wild

Venters, Vic, 110

Viviparous Quadrupeds of North America, 135

Walker, R.J., 31

Warbler, 152; Audubon's, 153; cerulean, 152; Kirtland's, 153; myrtle, 151, 152; palm, 158; pine, 158; yellow-rumped, 153-55, 158

Warner Valley, 137

Washington-Slagbaai National Park, Bonaire, 24

Weaver, Keith, 105, 108

Wheeler, Bill, 169

Wilcox, Bruce, 8

Wilcox, Peter, 95

Wilderness Act of 1964, 127, 167

Wilderness Society, 167

Wildlife: active versus passive management of, 166, 167, 174-76; participants in recreation involving, 179

Wildlife in North Carolina, 110

Wilson, Edward O., 7, 8, 23, 112, 178, 181, 183, 184

Winnebago Marsh, 163

Winnebago Tribe, 163

Wisconsin Department of Natural Resources, 169

Wolf, gray, 135-37

Wood Buffalo National Park, 5
Woods Hole Biological Laboratory, 72

Yukon Flats National Wildlife Refuge,
    159
Yosemite National Park, 3, 4

Zooplankton, 19, 20